THE PEOPLE COULD FLY

American Black Folktales

THE PEOPLE COULD FLY

American Black Folktales

told by VIRGINIA HAMILTON

Illustrated by LEO *and* DIANE DILLON

SCHOLASTIC INC.
New York Toronto London Auckland Sydney

For my father,
Kenneth Hamilton,
and for all who've told the tale

ISBN 0-590-48211-4

12 11 10 9 8 7 6 5 4   4 5 6 7 8 9/9

Printed in the U.S.A.   14

First Scholastic printing, January 1994

Contents

Introduction

Folktales take us back to the very beginnings of people's lives, to their hopes and their defeats. American black folktales originated with peoples, most of whom long ago were brought from Africa to this country against their will. These peoples were torn from their individual cultures as they left the past, their families and their social groups, and their languages and customs behind.

The black peoples coming to America before the end of the Civil War entered as slaves, and they were separated and isolated by law because of their race. The African in them was forcibly suppressed by the white slaveowners.

They were not supposed to speak their own languages. The slaveowners made them speak American English but forbade them to learn to read or write it. They were compelled to do hard labor and exhorted never to run away. Alone and helpless, the slaves lived under conditions as brutal as any group of people has ever endured.

It is amazing that the former Africans could ever smile and laugh, let alone make up riddles and songs and jokes and tell tales. As slaves, they were forced to live without citizenship, without rights, as property—like horses and cows—belonging to someone else. But no amount of hard labor and suffering could suppress their powers of imagination.

Out of the contacts the plantation slaves made in their new world, combined with memories and habits from the old world of Africa, came a body of folk expression about the slaves and their experiences. The slaves created tales in which various animals—such as the rabbit, fox, bear, wolf, turtle or terrapin, snake, and possum—took on the characteristics of the people found in the new environment of the plantation. The rabbit, known as B'rabby and later called Brer, Buh, or Bruh Rabbit, became a particular favorite of the slave tellers. Rabbit was small and apparently helpless compared to the powerful bear, the wily fox, and the ferocious wolf. But the slave teller made the rabbit smart, tricky, and clever, the winner over larger and stronger animals. Still, Bruh Rabbit sometimes got into trouble, just as the slaves did, which made him seem all the more human. To the slaves, the rabbit came to be identified with themselves, which makes these tales highly unusual in the animal folklore genre.

Later on, probably after the Civil War, a slave character—usually called John—often took the place of Bruh Rabbit in the tales. John became the trickster hero who outwits Old Mas, the slaveowner, and wins his freedom. A group of slave narratives that were true tales of escape also developed, as did tales of magic, fantasy escape tales, and supernatural tales.

In the Cape Verde Islands off the coast of West Africa, slavery was abolished in 1876. Black Portuguese fishermen freely emigrated from the islands to America and they were unique in that they, too, had a history of slavery. They brought with them their highly individual folktales, some of which are included in this collection.

Black folktales were first recorded in the late nineteenth century. In 1880, journalist Joel Chandler Harris collected some of the oral literature of the slaves in *Uncle Remus: His Songs and His Sayings*. Many Americans' first exposure to black folktales came through the character of elderly Uncle Remus, the slave who had a favored position on the old plantation. Harris' Uncle Remus told animal tales in fractured English to the little white boy of the plantation house. But author Harris was not concerned with reproducing exactly the tales or their language. Harris and his contemporaries used phonetic dialect as a literary device. They felt that an exaggerated colloquial language best symbolized what they regarded as the quaint appeal of lowly, rural people.

Thus, some of the folktales recorded by early collectors are much more difficult to read than the narratives in the form of letters and petitions that some slaves managed to write themselves. But gradually, collectors attempted to express the tales in a more realistic, readable fashion. When Black English, such as Gullah (Angola) English, was used, a glossary was added.

The tales in this collection are in four sections that represent the main body of black folktales. I use a reasonably colloquial language or dialect, depending on the folktale. Moderate colloquialisms are understandable and readable. They reflect the expressiveness of the original slave teller, and later the free black storyteller.

Remember that these folktales were once a creative way for an oppressed people to express their fears and hopes to one another. They lend themselves well to being read out loud, as they were told out loud so long ago. They can be enjoyed by young and old alike.

Remember also that these tales, like all folktales, belong to all of us. They are part of our American tradition and part of the history of our country. They show you how I tell the black folktales. For they are told in my own voice, echoing the voices of slaves and fugitives, some of whom are my ancestors. To this very day, folktales are being told, altered, retold, and made. A tale naturally changes as it is told by one person to another.

These tales were created out of sorrow. But the hearts and minds of the black people who formed them, expanded them, and passed them on to us were full of love and hope. We must look on the tales as a celebration of the human spirit.

Remember the voices from the past. As do the folktales, keep close all the past that was good, and that remains full of promise.

Virginia Hamilton

Yellow Springs, Ohio
April 1985

THE PEOPLE COULD FLY

American Black Folktales

HE LION, BRUH BEAR, AND BRUH RABBIT

And Other Animal Tales

He Lion, Bruh Bear, and Bruh Rabbit

Say that he Lion would get up each and every mornin. Stretch and walk around. He'd roar, "ME AND MYSELF. ME AND MYSELF," like that. Scare all the little animals so they were afraid to come outside in the sunshine. Afraid to go huntin or fishin or whatever the little animals wanted to do.

"What we gone do about it?" they asked one another. Squirrel leapin from branch to branch, just scared. Possum playin dead, couldn't hardly move him.

He Lion just went on, stickin out his chest and roarin, "ME AND MYSELF. ME AND MYSELF."

The little animals held a sit-down talk, and one by one and two by two and all by all, they decide to go see Bruh Bear and Bruh Rabbit. For they know that Bruh Bear been around. And Bruh Rabbit say he has, too.

So they went to Bruh Bear and Bruh Rabbit. Said, "We have some trouble. Old he Lion, him scarin everybody, roarin every mornin and all day, 'ME AND MYSELF. ME AND MYSELF,' like that."

"Why he Lion want to do that?" Bruh Bear said.

"Is that all he Lion have to say?" Bruh Rabbit asked.

"We don't know why, but that's all he Lion can tell us and we didn't ask him to tell us that," said the little animals. "And him scarin the children with it. And we wish him to stop it."

"Well, I'll go see him, talk to him. I've known he Lion a long kind of time," Bruh Bear said.

"I'll go with you," said Bruh Rabbit. "I've known he Lion most long as you."

That bear and that rabbit went off through the forest. They kept hearin somethin. Mumble, mumble. Couldn't make it out. They got farther in the forest. They heard it plain now. "ME AND MYSELF. ME AND MYSELF."

"Well, well, well," said Bruh Bear. He wasn't scared. He'd been around the whole forest, seen a lot.

"My, my, my," said Bruh Rabbit. He'd seen enough to know not to be afraid of an old he lion. Now old he lions could be dangerous, but you had to know how to handle them.

The bear and the rabbit climbed up and up the cliff where he Lion

had his lair. They found him. Kept their distance. He watchin them and they watchin him. Everybody actin cordial.

"Hear tell you are scarin everybody, all the little animals, with your roarin all the time," Bruh Rabbit said.

"I roars when I pleases," he Lion said.

"Well, might could you leave off the noise first thing in the mornin, so the little animals can get what they want to eat and drink?" asked Bruh Bear.

"Listen," said he Lion, and then he roared: "ME AND MYSELF. ME AND MYSELF. Nobody tell me what not to do," he said. "I'm the king of the forest, *me and myself.*"

"Better had let me tell you somethin," Bruh Rabbit said, "for I've seen Man, and I know him the real king of the forest."

He Lion was quiet awhile. He looked straight through that scrawny lil Rabbit like he was nothin atall. He looked at Bruh Bear and figured he'd talk to him.

"You, Bear, you been around," he Lion said.

"That's true," said old Bruh Bear. "I been about everywhere. I've been around the whole forest."

"Then you must know somethin," he Lion said.

"I know lots," said Bruh Bear, slow and quiet-like.

"Tell me what you know about Man," he Lion said. "He think him the king of the forest?"

"Well, now, I'll tell you," said Bruh Bear, "I been around, but I haven't ever come across Man that I know of. Couldn't tell you nothin about him."

So he Lion had to turn back to Bruh Rabbit. He didn't want to but he had to. "So what?" he said to that lil scrawny hare.

"Well, you got to come down from there if you want to see Man," Bruh Rabbit said. "Come down from there and I'll show you him."

He Lion thought a minute, an hour, and a whole day. Then, the next day, he came on down.

He roared just once, "ME AND MYSELF. ME AND MYSELF. Now," he said, "come show me Man."

So they set out. He Lion, Bruh Bear, and Bruh Rabbit. They go along and they go along, rangin the forest. Pretty soon, they come to a clearin. And playin in it is a little fellow about nine years old.

"Is that there Man?" asked he Lion.

"Why no, that one is called Will Be, but it sure is not Man," said Bruh Rabbit.

So they went along and they went along. Pretty soon, they come upon a shade tree. And sleepin under it is an old, olden fellow, about ninety years olden.

"There must lie Man," spoke he Lion. "I knew him wasn't gone be much."

"That's not Man," said Bruh Rabbit. "That fellow is Was Once. You'll know it when you see Man."

So they went on along. He Lion is gettin tired of strollin. So he roars, "ME AND MYSELF. ME AND MYSELF." Upsets Bear so that Bear doubles over and runs and climbs a tree.

"Come down from there," Bruh Rabbit tellin him. So after a while Bear comes down. He keepin his distance from he Lion, anyhow.

And they set out some more. Goin along quiet and slow.

In a little while they come to a road. And comin on way down the road, Bruh Rabbit sees Man comin. Man about twenty-one years old. Big and strong, with a big gun over his shoulder.

"There!" Bruh Rabbit says. "See there, he Lion? There's Man. You better go meet him."

"I will," says he Lion. And he sticks out his chest and he roars, "ME AND MYSELF. ME AND MYSELF." All the way to Man he's roarin proud, "ME AND MYSELF, ME AND MYSELF!"

"Come on, Bruh Bear, let's go!" Bruh Rabbit says.

"What for?" Bruh Bear wants to know.

"You better come on!" And Bruh Rabbit takes ahold of Bruh Bear and half drags him to a thicket. And there he makin the Bear hide with him.

For here comes Man. He sees old he Lion real good now. He drops to one knee and he takes aim with his big gun.

Old he Lion is roarin his head off: "ME AND MYSELF! ME AND MY-SELF!"

The big gun goes off: PA-LOOOM!

He Lion falls back hard on his tail.

The gun goes off again. PA-LOOOM!

He Lion is flyin through the air. He lands in the thicket.

"Well, did you see Man?" asked Bruh Bear.

"I seen him," said he Lion. "Man spoken to me unkind, and got a great long stick him keepin on his shoulder. Then Man taken that stick down and him speakin real mean. Thunderin at me and light-

nin comin from that stick, awful bad. Made me sick. I had to turn
around. And Man pointin that stick again and thunderin at me some
more. So I come in here, cause it seem like him throwed some stick-
ers at me each time it thunder, too."

"So you've met Man, and you know zactly what that kind of him
is," says Bruh Rabbit.

"I surely do know that," he Lion said back.

Awhile after he Lion met Man, things were some better in the forest. Bruh Bear knew what Man looked like so he could keep out of

his way. That rabbit always did know to keep out of Man's way. The little animals could go out in the mornin because he Lion was more peaceable. He didn't walk around roarin at the top of his voice all the time. And when he Lion did lift that voice of his, it was like, "Me and Myself and Man. Me and Myself and Man." Like that.

Wasn't too loud atall.

Animal tales are the most widely known black folktales. Because of the menial labor slaves were made to do, they observed and came to know many kinds of animals throughout their daily lives. They developed a keen interest in these lowly creatures. Because they had so little knowledge about the fauna they found here, they made up tales that to some extent explained and fit their observations of animal behavior. Furthermore, the tales satisfied the slaves' need to explain symbolically and secretly the ruling behavior of the slaveowners in relation to themselves. As time passed, the tales were told more for entertainment and instruction.

"He Lion, Bruh Bear, and Bruh Rabbit" is a typical tale of an animal, whether it is wolf, lion, bear, rabbit, goat, tiger, etc., that learns through experience to fear man. It is the rabbit that shows man to the lion. And the rabbit, representing the slave in the animal tales, knows from experience to fear man. The tale ranges throughout North and South America, Europe, and Africa.

Doc Rabbit, Bruh Fox, and Tar Baby

Heard tell about Doctor Rabbit and Brother Fox. They were buildin a house. And they kept a crock of cream in the bubbly brook down below the house they were buildin. Every once in a while, Doc Rabbit got thirsty. And he hollered aside so Bruh Fox wouldn't know who it was, "Whooo-hooo, whooo-hooo, whooo-hooo," like that. Scared Bruh Fox to death.

"Who is it there?" Bruh Fox say.

"Sounds like somebody callin bad," said Doc Rabbit.

"Well, can you tell what they want?" Bruh Fox say.

"Can't tell nothin and I'm not lookin to see," said Doc.

"Oh, but yer the doctor. Yer the doctor, you'd better go see," says Bruh Fox.

So Doc Rabbit went off down to the bubbly brook where the water ribbled, keepin the cream cold. He drank a long drink of sweet cream. Then he went back to help Bruh Fox with the house.

"Who was it callin?" asks Bruh Fox.

"Just started callin me, was all it was," said Doc Rabbit.

So Doc Rabbit got down to work. But the sun was hot and he came thirsty again. He went about callin out the side of his mouth:

"Whoo-ahhh, whooo-ahhh, whoo-ahhh!"

"Who is callin so scared?" says Bruh Fox, trembly all over.

"Somebody callin me for help, I expect," Doc Rabbit said. "But I am sure not goin this time, me."

"You have to go. You have to, yer the only doctor. Go ahead on, you," Bruh Fox say.

Big Doc Rabbit went down to the brook again. The water was so cool and ribbly and it kept the crock of cream so fresh and cold. Doc Rabbit drank about half of the cream this time. Then he went back up to help Brother Fox with the hard labor of raisin the roof.

Bruh Fox says, "What was the name of the one callin you this time?"

"Name of about half done callin," mumbled Doc Rabbit. "Whew! This work is a hard labor."

The rabbit toiled and sweated until his fur was wringin wet. He took off his fur coat, too. He wrung it dry and put it back on. But that didn't even cool him any. He says over his shoulder, says,

"Whooo-wheee, whooo-wheee!" like that.

The fox says, lookin all around, "Somebody else callin you, Rabbit."

"I sure am not goin this time," Doc Rabbit said. "I'll just stay right here this time."

"You go on," says Bruh Fox. "Go ahead on, folks needin you today."

So Doc Rabbit scurried down to the ribblin brook. It was nice by the water. He sat himself down, took up the crock of cream. He drank it all down. Then he ran off.

Fox feel a suspicion. He went down there, saw the cream was all gone. He filled up the crock with some lemon and sugar water he had. He knew Rabbit was after anything cold and sweet.

"Think I'll catch me a doctor and a hare together," Fox says to himself.

Next, he made a little baby out of the tar there. The baby lookin just like a baby rabbit. He named it Tar Baby and sat it right there on the waterside. Bruh Fox went back up the hill and he worked on his house. He thought he might keep the house to himself. Doc Rabbit was bein bad so and not workin atall.

Doc Rabbit came back for a drink. He spied the new crock full. And he spied Tar Baby just sittin, gazin out on the water.

"What you doin here, baby rabbit?" Rabbit asked Tar Baby.

Tar Baby wouldn't say. Too stuck up.

"You better speak to me," Doc Rabbit said, "or I'll have to hurt you."

But the Tar Baby wasn't gone speak to a stranger.

So Doc Rabbit kicked Tar Baby with his left hind foot. Foot got stuck, it did. "Whoa, turn me loose!" the rabbit cried. "Turn me loose!"

Tar Baby stayed still. Gazin at the water. Lookin out over the ribbly water.

So Doc Rabbit kicked hard with his right hind foot. "Oh, oh, I'm stuck again. You'd better let me loose, baby," Doc Rabbit said. "I got another good foot to hit you with."

Tar Baby said nothin. Gazin at the water. Lookin far on by the waterside.

Doc Rabbit kicked Tar Baby with another foot, and that foot got stuck way deep. "Better turn me loose," Rabbit hollered, gettin scared now. Shakin now. Says, "I got one foot left and here it comes!"

He kicked that tar baby with the one foot left, and that got stuck just like the other three.

"Well, well, well," said Doc Rabbit, shakin his head and lookin at Tar Baby.

Tar Baby gazin on the water. Watchin out for the pretty birds.

"Well, I still got my head," Doc Rabbit said. "I'm mad, now! I'm agone use my head, too."

He used his head on the little tar baby. Butted his head in the tar baby's stomach as hard as he could. Doc Rabbit's head got stuck clear up to his eyes. His big rabbit ears went whole in the tar of Tar Baby.

That was the way Bruh Fox found him. Doc Rabbit was stuck in Tar Baby. Bruh Fox got him loose.

"What must I do with you?" Bruh Fox said. He led Rabbit along to the house they were buildin. "You the one drank up my crock of cream. I didn't get one taste. Have a mind to burn you in a fire, too."

"Oh, I like fires," Doc Rabbit said. "Do go on burn me up, Bruh Fox, for it's my pleasure to have my coat on fire."

"Well, then, I won't burn you," said the fox. "Burnin up is too good for you."

"Huh," grunted Doc Rabbit. He said no more. Bruh Fox had him in his mouth, a-danglin down his back. Then he laid the rabbit under his paws so he could speak.

"Well, think I'll throw you in that thorny briar patch," Bruh Fox said. "How you like that?"

"Oh, mercy, don't do that!" cried Doc Rabbit. "Whatever you do with me, don't dare throw me in those thorny briars!"

"That's what I'll do, then," Bruh Fox said.

And that's what Brother Fox did. He sure did. Took Doc Rabbit by the short hair and threw him—*Whippit! Whappit!*—right in the briar patch.

"Hot lettuce pie! This is where I want to be," Doc Rabbit hollered for happiness. He was square in the middle of the briar patch. "Here is where my mama and papa had me born and raised. Safe at last!"

"Didn't know rabbits have they homes in the briars," Bruh Fox said, scratching his tail.

He knows it now.

There are some three hundred versions of the Tar Baby tale. Variants of the tale appear in many countries. In the Bahamas the elephant creates the tar baby; in Brazil an old woman or man traps a monkey in a sticky wax baby. There is a version from India, and there are African versions among the Ewes and Yorubas, all showing the great antiquity and universality of this tale.

Long ago, in certain localities of Georgia, the tar baby was considered an actual, living, monstrous creature. The monster was composed of tar and haunted isolated places on the plantation. It would insult people to the point at which they would strike out at it and thus become trapped in its sticky substance.

Tappin, the Land Turtle

Once a time, there was land chil'ren and tree chil'ren. And there was the land turtle, he call isself Tappin. Tappin has six chil'ren. They all hungry. Everybody hungry all on the land, for it was famine time.

There was the eagle up there, hidin in a cloud. He on his way cross the ocean. He go for the palm oil and the seed to feed his tree chil'ren.

Tappin see what the eagle do and he say, "Hold on there. It bein hard times, where you come by all this and that to feed your tree chil'ren? I got six of my own. Show me where you get your food."

Eagle says, "I has to fly cross the ocean to get this and that."

Tappin, he say, "You give me some of them wings you got, and I'll travel with you."

Eagle, he say, "All right. When you wanter go?"

Tappin tell him, "The first cock crow, tomorry mornin." So first cock crow gone come. But Tappin, he not wait for it. It be three o'clock and Tappin go over to Eagle's house. Sayin, "Cuckoo-coo, cuckoo-coo."

Eagle tell him, "You go on back home. Lay you down, itaint day yet."

But Tappin kept it up, "Cuckoo-coo."

So Eagle gets on up, say, "What you want now?"

Tappin tell him, "Put me three feathers on this side and three on the other side."

So the eagle, he pull out the feathers for Tappin. He put three on one side of Tappin's shell and three on the other. Now, Eagle say, "Lemme see you fly."

So Tappin, he right off start in to fly. One of the feathers fall off him.

"That be all right," he says. "I got me some more wings. Let's be on our way."

So Eagle and Tappin flew and they flew. But over the ocean all of Tappin's eagle feathers fall off. Tappin commence fallin in the water. He fallin fast when Eagle go catch him and put him under his wing.

"Whew!" Tappin say. "It do smell *foul* under here."

Eagle let him drop in the ocean. Tappin fall down and down under water, way down to the underworld.

The king down there, king of the underworld, meet up with Tappin. He say, say, "Why you here? What you doin here?"

Tappin tell him, say, "King, we have terrible time on the earth. We can't get nothin to eat. I got six land chil'ren and I can't find food for them. The eagle, he got but three tree chil'ren and he can fly cross the ocean and get all the food he want. So would you please gimme somethin to feed my chil'ren?"

King tell him, "Aw-right, aw-right." He give Tappin a dipper, long-handle cup. He tell Tappin, "Take this, and when you want food for your chil'ren, say this:

"Bakon coleh

Bakon cawbey

Bakon cawhubo lebe lebe."

So Tappin, he carry home the dipper and he go to the chil'ren. "Come on here," he say to them. When they all come on here, he say this:

"Bakon coleh

Bakon cawbey

Bakon cawhubo lebe lebe."

There is everythin in the dipper. There is gravy, biscuit, and meat. The chil'ren have plenty to eat now.

So Tappin, he says to isself, "I'll sell this dipper to my own king."
So he show the dipper to his own king and he say:

"*Bakon coleh*
Bakon cawbey
Bakon cawhubo lebe lebe."

There the food come out the dipper. They get everythin to eat. So
the king go and call all the people and everybody eat from the dipper.
They ate and ate the meat, the fruit, everythin. Tappin think he take
the dipper back home, so he do.

"Come on, chil'ren," Tappin say. He tryin to feed them but nothin
comin from the dipper. Nothin. So when the dipper out, it's out.

Tappin say, "Aw-right, I'll go to the king of the underworld and
have him fix this dipper up."

He go way down to the underworld and he say to the king there,
"King, what is the matter? I can't feed the land chil'ren no more."

King say, "You take this cowhide, and when you want somethin,
you say:

"*Sheet n-oun*
n-jacko
nou o quaako."

So Tappin, he does it. But that cowhide start to beat the land
chil'ren. It say, "Drop, drop." Some children are dead. Some is only
sick. But they all drop down.

Tappin, he say, "I'll call the underworld king up here." He calls the king and all the people. And he has isself a cover made to fit him before he have the cowhide to beat. He make cover of sand and some lime, to cover him good. Then, he say:

"Sheet n-oun
n-jacko
nou o quaako."

The cowhide beat and beat. It beat everybody—it beat the king, too. It beat, beat, and beat right through the cover over Tappin. Tappin have beat signs all on his back. Why, Tappin's shell have marks on it all over to this day.

And that's why you never find Tappin in a clean place. You look, see him under some leaves or a log lyin there. That's Tappin, beat marks all on he shell.

This tale was first told by Cujo Lewis of Plateau, Alabama, and recorded in heavy dialect. He was brought to America on a slave ship from the west coast of Africa in 1859. It was the custom among some of the African peoples to name a child after the day on which he or she was born. Cujo means Monday.

Tappin is a dialect word for *terrapin,* the American dry-land turtle. There were African animal prototypes, such as the jackal, the hare, and the tortoise, for the American black folktales. The jackal survived in the tales as the fox; the hare as the rabbit, and the tortoise as the dry-land turtle or terrapin.

This tale includes examples of African words in verse that were meant to make magic. Their meaning, unfortunately, is lost to us.

Bruh Alligator and Bruh Deer

Long time, nothin here but animal and bird and the Indian. Bruh Alligator and Bruh Deer not any kind of friends atall. Bruh Alligator even plan to kill Bruh Deer when he get the chance. And Bruh Deer very afraid to swim cross the river. Whenever he go down to the river edge for a drink, he cock his head, listenin, and look all around him before he do drink. Just so scared, he, of Bruh Alligator.

By and by comes the *buckras,* the white owners. And then comes the black slaves; and by and by, the *buckras* fetch the hounds. And then the Indian is gone and the *buckras* come to hunt Bruh Deer with they English beagle hounds. They dogs, they beagle hounds, they so swift and they tryin to get so close to Bruh Deer. Only chance Bruh Deer has is to take to the water. But who in the water? Bruh Alligator, who. Nothin matter to Bruh Deer. He have to make for the water when the hounds come too close.

Now the first time the *buckras* run Bruh Deer with the hounds, he didn't know nothin about them. And he just lie down in his bed in the thicket on the edge of the broom-grass field. But here come the hounds, and Bruh Deer so afraid and so, he jump and he run. And he gets away to the river first. Just as he ready to jump off the bluff above the river, he look down and see Bruh Alligator's two big eyes come risin out of the water. Bruh Alligator just waitin for him!

That alligator hungry. Vittles very scarce that time a season. His belly be pinchin him hard, now. But Bruh Deer is fat, and so he is in heavy trouble. The alligator there in front of him. The beagles there behind him. What Bruh Deer gone do? He sees the alligator and he hears the beagles.

Bruh Deer make a sudden twist to the side just before the hounds see him. He burn the wind down the riverbank below the bluff, and he cross the water where Bruh Alligator never see him.

Here come the beagles boilin hard for the bluff. They come so fast upon Bruh Deer's track, they never have a chance to stop. Two or three go on over the bluff, and they drop in the water right in front of Bruh Alligator's snout.

Bruh Alligator think to heself, What this here? I never seen such

animals before. But it's vittles! Food! And he grabs one, two of the beagles and pulls them under the water. The other hound swum out of there, took he feet in he hands, and ripped on home.

Well, Bruh Deer got away that time. He gone! And when he ready to cross that river again, he look around for Bruh Alligator first. He find him, too. Bruh Alligator stretched out on a mudbank in the sunhot. He got a belly full of beagle and he satisfy with heself. He sound asleep. And Bruh Deer sneak close to the river to take a chance on gettin across.

Before Bruh Deer can wet he hoof, Bruh Alligator see him and he slip off the bank to go meet Bruh Deer. How Bruh Deer gone get across go see his family? Before he even thinkin about it, Bruh Alligator start a-talkin.

"Brutha," Bruh Alligator say, "this thing that I ate they call beagle is very good vittles. I love eatin him very much, too. He so easy to catch, and he got no horns to scratch my throat."

"Well, if you love eatin him so and you want to catch him so, will you leave me and my family alone?" Bruh Deer ask him.

Bruh Alligator answer, "I can't catch the beagle less he fall in the river. So let's you, me, make a greement to last as long as this river run."

"What is the greement?" ask Bruh Deer.

"Here tis," says Bruh Alligator. "When you take to the river, I'll take the beagle what chasin you. Me for you, and you for me, and both us for one another."

So Bruh Deer say it all right with him.

And that how it been since the greement made. Whenever hounds run Bruh Deer, Bruh Deer take to the river and Bruh Alligator leave him alone. The hound gone track Deer, and Alligator gone get hound.

But if Bruh Deer ever come to the river without the dogs chasin him, then he have to take he chance.

This tale is translated from the Gullah dialect. In Gullah, the last two paragraphs of the tale above would read: "Dat w'ymekso ebbuh sence de' 'greement mek, w'enebbuh dog run'um, buh deer tek de ribbuh en' buh alligettuh lem'lone, en' w'en de beagle' come 'e ketch'um, but ef buh deer ebbuh come duh ribbuh bidout dog dey att'um, him haffuh tek 'e chance."

Bruh Lizard and Bruh Rabbit

Don't know some animal tells. Hear um but forget um. Do know about Bruh Lizard and Bruh Rabbit, though. You never hear um tell how Bruh Lizard bested Bruh Rabbit? Well, that lizard was a hard worker. He had a big sword he use to cut his crop. Sword knew how to work by heself and it cut so fine, there was nothin left, once somethin was cut. Bruh Lizard speakin words to the sword and Sword do all the work. That's how it went.

Now, Bruh Rabbit, he is smart. He don't have him a sword like the lizard has, and he wants one. So he hides behind a bush and he watches Sword workin for Bruh Lizard. He wants it very bad, too.

One day Bruh Lizard has to go away. And Bruh Rabbit, he sneak up and he steal Bruh Lizard's sword. Bruh Rabbit laughs to heself because he now got Sword. He think he knows the words that Lizard says to Sword, so he calls out, "Go-ee-tell," like that. And Sword starts in workin, just a-cuttin and a-slashin this way and that and all around.

Pretty soon, old Sword finish up the crop and the rabbit want it to stop. Sword is comin very close to the other crop the rabbit is keepin to live on.

So Bruh Rabbit, he yells out to Sword, "Go-ee-tell. Go-ee-tell!" like that. That just make Sword work that much faster. Sword go on and cut down everythin Rabbit have. It don't leave nothin, not one leaf cabbage.

Now Bruh Lizard, he been hidin behind a bush. He sees the whole thing. He is laughin and laughin to heself at Bruh Rabbit, cause that Rabbit think he so smart when he steal Sword. And now Bruh Rabbit got nothin to eat all winter long.

Bruh Rabbit spies the lizard, and he calls over there, "Lizard, Bruh, stop Sword!"

Bruh Lizard, he call right back, "It my Sword."

Bruh Rabbit, he say then, "That's so. It's your Sword, but please stop it. It ain't got no sense. It cut down everythin I got."

Lizard say, "Sword work faster every time he hear 'Go-ee-tell.'" The lizard laughs again, and he calls out real loud, "Go-ee-pom!" Sword stop.

The lizard grinnin to heself all over the place. Then he slide out there and pick up Sword and take it on home.

Rabbit watch him go.

That's all.

A version of a dialect plantation tale from the Georgia Sea Isles. It is a derivation of the numerous magic-hoe motif tales from Africa and Europe. This is one of the few animal tales in which the cunning Bruh Rabbit doesn't come out the winner.

In another version of the magic-hoe tale, Bruh Rabbit and Bruh Wolf are the contestants. The rabbit's saying "Swish, swish" makes the hoe go faster. When the wolf says "Slow, boy," the hoe slows down.

Bruh Alligator Meets Trouble

A Gullah Dialect Tale

Bruh Rabbit has words with Bruh Gator on account Bruh Gator can't keep he mouth shut. He tell Bruh Rabbit one day, tellum say, "We gators live in the river and my chil'ren smart cause of that. Bruh Rabbit, I can't see how *oonuh* can live *pontop* the hard land. Can't stand the land, myself." Say all that to Bruh Rabbit, and the rabbit dint think much of the gator for it.

Bruh Rabbit just say, "Mebbe you right, Bruh Gator. We on the land seein a lot a trouble."

"What Trouble is?" asked Bruh Gator.

Bruh Rabbit can't believe it. "You sayin you never know trouble yet?"

"Never know nothin about him," Bruh Gator say. "How just do Trouble look? How him stand?"

It then Bruh Rabbit catch on. He know a way to shut he Gator mouth about them is livin on land. He show Bruh Gator he place and have fun with him besides.

"Don't know can tell you how Trouble lookin, Bruh Gator, nor how he standin. But maybe I can show you him, you get on come tomorra," Bruh Rabbit say.

"That be fine," say Bruh Gator. And he go slide under the river water out of sight.

Next time, Bruh Gator up before *dayclean.* He fixin he up, him, ready get on with Bruh Rabbit.

Sis Alligator, she wake up sheself and she *quizzit* Bruh Gator, "Where you goin to?"

Bruh Gator, he don't bother *crack he teeth* at Sis Alligator. He go on long fixin up heself.

Bruh Gator and Sis Alligator and all they little alligators is *buckras*—they wears *berry* white skins all over from they heads to they tails, for true. And Bruh Gator right now see in the mirra he skin lookin good.

"I say," Sis Alligator say, "where you goin to?"

Now Bruh Gator see there's no gettin around Sis Alligator, so he has to tell, say, "I'm goin aroun with Bruh Rabbit."

"What for you goin aroun with Bruh Rabbit?" *quizzit* Sis Alligator.

Bruh Gator dint want say, but he have to so he tell her, say, "I am goin for to meet Trouble."

"What Trouble is?" asked Sis Alligator.

"I ask Bruh Rabbit that," say Bruh Gator, "and he say, '*Enteh comepon* Trouble sometime?' And I tell him no, *nuh* me. And so, that what I go for *shum*," Bruh Gator say.

"Well, I want to *shum* and go along, too," Sis Alligator tell him.

It take a while, but finally Bruh Gator tell her she can't come. She beggin and beggin, but she can't come with Bruh Gator and Bruh Rabbit.

"Oh, go long then," she tell him, and he do so. Him don't know she gone follow and she chil'ren gone follow she. And Sis Alligator never know until be too late them follow she.

Bruh Gator go on along. He look this side and that side but he can't find Bruh Rabbit. Now Bruh Rabbit be right there, hidin. He smokin he pipe. He wait for Bruh Gator get heself in the broom-grass field. He wait.

And Bruh Gator get tired, lookin. He *comepon* the broom grass, it tall and dry. He tired out. He stretch heself out in the broom grass, smell nice. And he fall heself asleep.

Bruh Rabbit think now Bruh Gator asleep. He tippin right *pontop* and *'e shum he yeye.* And they shut tight, and that rabbit know Bruh Gator asleep for true.

So Bruh Rabbit say to heself, "Bruh Gator gone know what call Trouble this day."

But then he *yeddy* somethin. *He yeddy, but he ain't shum.* Then he

shum Sis Alligator and little alligators comin into the broom grass. They huntin Bruh Gator, but they don't find him. Him lyin too low in the high grass. They gets tired lookin. So they lays down just the same as Bruh Gator. They off on *turrah* side the broom-grass field. Sis Alligator dozin off, and the little ones find she and all curlum up, they tails touchin. And they all falls asleep.

Bruh Rabbit, *'e shum* and he say to heself, "They all of them gone know what call Trouble this day!"

Bruh Rabbit smells the wind. He find out which way it drivin. He knock the coal from he pipe. Red-hot coal fall in the broom grass. Bruh Rabbit blow on the coal and it catch fire. Fire set *pon* the field, the broom grass all around on fire. And Bruh Rabbit find heself a stump to set *pontop* and he set up there and he watch and wait. The fire comin strong all around and around, for true.

All wake up, smellin smoke. Bruh Alligator smell sumpthin on the smoke. Little alligators! He hurry on over *turrah* side the field. He find all them. He don't holler at them. He let it go.

Bruh Gator *yeddy* sumpthin snappin. "What's that?" he say.

And the wind cause a fire flare. It high and it red and bright. A little alligator shout out, "What's *that*!"

"It must be Trouble," says Bruh Gator.

And Sis Alligator *quizzit,* "That Trouble, for true?"

Well, the gator don't know for true. He live in mud and the river, how he gone know sumpthin? He never lay he *yeye* on fire, so he don't know what be there right all around smokin and flarin.

They all lookin at Trouble and think the fire so pretty.

"Keep still now," Bruh Gator say. "We don't want to scare Trouble away."

So they all be quiet. Until the fire flare real high and close. Sparks flyin, they *swinge* all over them gators bare, white skins. The gators *swink* close down but it don't do them no good. They got to move. The hot fire is real up now. It blister they tails and they snouts. And the gators are runnin away. Bruh Gator is in front, the little alligators is in the middle, and Sis Alligator comin on from the last.

Bruh Rabbit see it all from he stump. He almost fall off, he laughin heself so much.

"Bruh Gator!" Bruh Rabbit shout hard. "*Ki!* Now you know how

Trouble look and how he stand! Don't go near him again. Go on back in the muddy river where you place is!"

All them alligators fall in the river, heads over heels. They so hot-boiled, the water go *swiiishshsh-pssst* when they hit it and steam come up like fog.

Bruh Gator tail hurt bad. He head and all he skin ache him. Sis Alligator and the little alligators, all same way. The water do cool them. It take them a whole day to get hold theyselves. *N'young* alligators cryin so.

Bruh Gator raise heself *pontop* the water and he yells loud as he can.

"Bruh Rabbit, I know was you bring Trouble for us alligators. You go on long today. But if I ever catch you near the river, I'll learn you how to come fool long me."

And to this *berry* day, Bruh Rabbit afraid of the alligators and the river.

But the alligators, they get out the water and what they find? They white skin is all burned black and crinkly up. They rough-lookin like wood bark. From then on, Bruh Gator have a horny hide—all gators do, too.

Never again do Bruh Gator sleep most far from the riverside. If he *yeddy* any branch creak, or bush snap, if he *yeddy* any sound be like cracklin fire, he don't say nothin. Just quick, him fall off he log in the water. Cause he know Trouble when he hear it. For true.

GLOSSARY FOR GULLAH WORDS

oonuh / you

pontop / upon top of

dayclean / dawn

quizzit / question closely

crack he teeth / a contemptuous, whistling inhalation

buckras / white people, slave slang, also meaning one of encompassing power

berry / very

enteh / ain't you, haven't you

comepon / come upon

nuh / not

shum / see

'e shum he yeye / he sees his eyes

yeddy / hear

he yeddy, but he ain't shum / he hears him, her, it, but he doesn't see him, her, it

turrah / t'other or other

yeye (pron. yay-yays) / eyes

swinge / singe

swink / shrink

Ki! / exclamation of disgust and contempt

n'young / young

Gullah is a combination of American, West Indian, English, and African languages. At one time it was the most pronounced Black English dialect in America. It is still spoken in parts of lowland South Carolina. The word Gullah is thought to have meant originally one (a slave, an African) who came from Angola. This tale is told here in a very modified Gullah.

Wolf and Birds and the Fish-Horse

Think a sea wave left this tell on the doorstep. This, about one wolf and his nephew. They were having this dance out there across the water. And this nephew wanted to fool Wolf. So he told Wolf it was going to be a feast and not a dance.

Wolf found the birds, asked them to lend him feathers so he could go fly across to the feast. The birds did give him feathers. Wolf went on out there and the dance started up.

Wolf was angry when he saw there was a dance and not a feast. Wolf asked his nephew for something to eat.

Nephew said, "No, there's nothing to eat. This is no feast, it's a dance."

The first one to get up and dance was Black Crow.

Wolf gets awful loud, says, "Black Crow, you think you somebody! If you didn't always dig up folks' corn, you'd be fine."

Crow took back the feather he given to Wolf.

The next one to dance was ugly Vulture. Wolf had to go say,

"Vulture, you think you somebody! If you wasn't always lookin for dead goats and donkeys to eat, you might be just fine."

That made Vulture take back his feather, too.

Here comes to dance old Blue Jay. Wolf started, says, "Blue Jay, you think you somebody! Good thing you don't see that red mouth of yours. Without it, you'd be fine."

Blue Jay went ahead and took back his feather.

Dancing by came the Hawk. Old Wolf had to say, "You, Hawk, you think you somebody! If you weren't always huntin people's chickens, you'd be just fine."

Hawk snatched back his feather off of Wolf.

Just then Guinea Hen came by dancing. Wolf says, says, "Guinea Hen, you sure think you somebody! But you don't see your own skinny head. If it was bigger, you'd be just fine."

Guinea Hen took back her feather.

When the dance was over, everybody left. Wolf was all alone out there. All alone and awful hungry. No food. Wolf started up crying.

Then come swimmin by who they call Aunt Fish-Horse. See Wolf is out there near the water. Can't get home across it. She says to Wolf, "What is wrong with you, are you sick?"

Wolf says back, "The birds loan me feathers. I fly to the dance and after while, they take their feathers back. Then they left me all by myself out here."

Wolf says, "Aunt Fish-Horse, if you take me to my own place, I'll pay you for it."

"Well, jump on my back," she tells him. And so that's what Wolf

did. She took him on to his place by way of the water. Halfway there, Wolf notices that Aunt Fish-Horse has milk. He will take her milk from her as soon as they reach shore. And he does. At the beach he pulls out the milk. He left Aunt Fish-Horse crying on the beach.

There came Nephew passing by. "Why you cryin like that?" he asks Aunt Fish-Horse.

She tells him, "Wolf did it, Wolf tore out my milk."

"If you pay me, I'll put Wolf back into your hands," says Nephew.

"If you can do that," says Aunt Fish-Horse, "I'll give you whatever you want."

So Nephew headed for home. Halfway there, he starts in hollering.

"Get my knife and my bowl. Wife! Wife! There's a fish-horse lying on the beach waitin for me to kill it!"

Wolf heard the hollering. "It's mine!" he called to his nephew. "I left Aunt Fish-Horse lyin there to get my own knife and bowl. Don't you touch her, she's mine!"

Wolf hurries down to the beach with his knife and bowl and his wife, too. He grabs Aunt Fish-Horse to kill her. But she grabbed him back. Got him by the leg and pulled him into the sea with her.

Wolf's wife is crying at the sight.

"Don't cry," Wolf tells her. "Aunt Fish-Horse is just playing."

Aunt Fish-Horse dives to the bottom, stays a minute.

When Wolf is up again, his wife is still crying. "Don't cry like that while I'm still breathin," Wolf tells his wife.

Aunt Fish-Horse dives again, stays down a long time. She comes up, Wolf is choking. His wife is crying, still.

"Better . . . had cry now . . ." Wolf chokes and sputters to his wife. "For . . . Fish-Horse is killin me. . . ."

Aunt Fish-Horse dived to the bottom with Wolf.

Wolf came up two days ago. He was full of little fish. And sand. And water. Nephew caught the little fish.

They had a funeral for Wolf. I saw it go by. All his children cried for him. All his people did, too.

This is a version of a black folktale of African origin, one of hundreds of such tales first told in a Portuguese/Mandingo dialect. The tales were brought to the northeastern United States from the Cape Verde Islands by black Portuguese immigrants. The Cape Verde Island group was formerly a colony of Portugal and is now a Portuguese overseas province that lies some six hundred miles off the West African coast.

The immigrants from the Cape Verde Islands are descended from African slaves imported by the early Portuguese to work their plantations; from Europeans—the Portuguese; and from most of the principal types associated with the African continent, including Arab and Hamitic. They are also descended from enslaved Africans who were gathered on the islands to be shipped across the Atlantic. But the enslaved Africans were left there when the slave trade ended. The slave trade to the United States ended almost completely in 1864; it ended officially in 1870. Slavery ended in the Cape Verde Islands in 1876.

Similar tales told by the Cape Verde immigrants about birds taking back their feathers are found in Africa, in Jamaica, and among Amerindians.

The tale "Wolf and Birds and the Fish-Horse" is taken from the Wolf *(Lob')* and Nephew *(Tobinh')* cycle of tales, similar in intent to the Boukee (Monkey) and Rabbit cycle tales found in the Bahamas.

Fish-horse *(peix' cabal')* / also called
     fish-cow—A manatee or walrus.

THE BEAUTIFUL GIRL
OF THE MOON TOWER

*And Other Tales of the Real,
Extravagant, and Fanciful*

The Beautiful Girl of the Moon Tower

There was a son named Anton. He dreamed that a girl placed a handkerchief over his face. He woke up but he saw no one.

Anton told his mother what he had dreamed. His mother said, "Anton, you've dreamed of something enchanted."

A few days later Anton dreamed the dream again and it was exactly the same: A girl placed a handkerchief over his face.

"Anton," his mother said, "you dream of a girl who lives with her father in the tower of the moon."

Anton thought about how to get there, to the tower of the moon.

He started out. In the middle of a field he met an eagle, an ant, a lion, and a dove. The four were quarreling over dividing a dead ox. Anton was kind enough to divide it for them. The eagle, the ant, the lion, and the dove were grateful.

The eagle said to Anton, "Wherever you are in trouble, call for me like this, 'O Eagle that flies seven miles without tiring or sweating!'"

The ant said to him, "Wherever you are in trouble, call for me, 'O Ant that goes where nobody knows!'"

The lion said to him, "Wherever you are in trouble, call for me, 'O Lion, king of the animals!' And I will save you."

The dove said to him, "Wherever you are in trouble, call for me, 'O Dove that flies seven miles without tiring or sweating!' And I will save you."

Anton went and he went. And he kept on going. He came to a place where he did not know what to do. Then he called,

> *"Ai, ai! Make of me an eagle*
> *That flies seven miles without tiring or sweating."*

He turned into an eagle and he flew seven miles without tiring or sweating. Then Anton came to the house of Mother-of-the-Wind.

Mother-of-the-Wind said to him, "Good day, my grandson!"

"Good day, my grandmother," said Anton.

"Why do you come here?" she said to him. "This is a place nobody ever came to before. My son is very bad."

"I am looking for a girl who lives in the tower of the moon," Anton told Mother-of-the-Wind.

They heard a noise that sounded as though it was breaking the

trees. It was Wind coming home. When he arrived, he said, "My mother, I smell royal blood here."

"No, you don't smell royal blood," Wind's mother said. "Not here you don't, because not a creature comes here."

Then Anton called,

> *"Ai, ai! Make of me an ant*
> *That goes where nobody knows."*

And he turned into an ant. He hid in a crack of the door.

Wind said, "My mother, give me water, I'm thirsty. Give me food to eat, I'm hungry. I've been blowing through all the trees and past every house, all over the world. And now I am tired."

So Wind drank and he ate and he lay down, resting.

"Let me ask you something," said Wind's mother. "Do you know the way to the tower of the moon?"

"Oh, I came from there a minute ago," said Wind. "Anyone who goes there has to pass by the inhabitants of the moon."

Wind was full and he had rested, so he left to blow again. And he blew through the world.

Anton, who was an ant, called for Dove. He said,

> *"Ai, ai! Make of me a dove*
> *That flies seven miles without tiring or sweating."*

He turned into a dove. Anton flew and he flew, until he came to the inhabitants of the moon. He saw the tower of the moon. He flew to the window; he called for the ant:

"Ai, ai! Make of me an ant
   That goes where nobody knows."

And he turned into an ant again. He went straight to the beautiful
girl's room.

He said,

"Ai, ai! Make of me Anton."

When he spoke, Anton turned into himself.

The girl asked him, "What are you doing here?"

Anton answered, "I've come to get you to marry me."

"I cannot marry you," she said. "My father will not let me."

"If there is no other way," said Anton, "I will take your father's
life. Go ask him where his life is." Then he called for the ant:

> *"Ai, ai! Make of me an ant*
> *That goes where nobody knows."*

The ant went under the father's bed.

The girl came there to her father. She asked him, "My father, where is your life?"

Her father said, "Why do you ask me? It is for some bedevilment."

"No, I only want to know," she said.

"Well," he said to her, "my life is inside the belly of a hog in my garden. Inside the hog's belly is an egg. Inside the egg is my life."

The ant that was Anton had been listening, and he said,

> *"Ai, ai! Make of me a boy."*

Anton turned into himself. He went to the girl's room. He said to her, "Now I'm going to kill that hog.

> *"Ai, ai! Make of me an eagle*
> *That flies seven miles without tiring or sweating."*

He turned into an eagle. He flew to the father's garden. He fought with the hog, but he could not get the better of it. So he called for the lion, said,

> *"Ai, ai! Make of me a lion,*
> *King of the animals."*

He turned into a lion. He fought with the hog. As soon as he began to fight, the father of the girl became sick. The more Anton beat the hog, the sicker the father became.

Finally, Anton killed the hog. He opened it up and took out the egg. He broke the egg and the father died. Anton called for the dove, saying,

> *"Ai, ai! Make of me a dove*
> *That flies seven miles without tiring or sweating."*

He became a dove. He flew to the window of the tower, where he turned into the ant, and he went inside. The house was covered in black. They buried the father.

As himself, Anton married the girl. He became king of the inhabitants of the moon. And the beautiful girl of the tower became queen.

Exaggerated-reality tales such as "The Beautiful Girl of the Moon Tower" stand apart from most folktales because of the individuality of their characterization and setting. They seem to be real or true and they present to us real people. However, there are elements in them that can only be called fanciful or extravagant. This tale from the Cape Verde Islands, told by Cape Verde Island immigrants to America, is one of a series of Anton tales with "his life in an egg" and transformation motifs. Anton, a symbol of the poor and weak, triumphs with the help of animals and magic, and with the beautiful young woman as reward.

Tales translated from the Portuguese and Cape Verde dialects are far less colloquial than the majority of black folktales. This may be due to some extent to the translation and also to the isolation of the Portuguese group in New England.

A Wolf and Little Daughter

One day Little Daughter was pickin some flowers. There was a fence around the house she lived in with her papa. Papa didn't want Little Daughter to run in the forest, where there were wolves. He told Little Daughter never to go out the gate alone.

"Oh, I won't, Papa," said Little Daughter.

One mornin her papa had to go away for somethin. And Little Daughter thought she'd go huntin for flowers. She just thought it wouldn't harm anythin to peep through the gate. And that's what she did. She saw a wild yellow flower so near to the gate that she stepped outside and picked it.

Little Daughter was outside the fence now. She saw another pretty flower. She skipped over and got it, held it in her hand. It smelled sweet. She saw another and she got it, too. Put it with the others. She was makin a pretty bunch to put in her vase for the table. And so Little Daughter got farther and farther away from the cabin. She picked the flowers, and the whole time she sang a sweet song.

All at once Little Daughter heard a noise. She looked up and saw a great big wolf. The wolf said to her, in a low, gruff voice, said, "Sing that sweetest, goodest song again."

So the little child sang it, sang,

"Tray-bla, tray-bla, cum qua, kimo."

And, *pit-a-pat, pit-a-pat, pit-a-pat, pit-a-pat,* Little Daughter tiptoed toward the gate. She's goin back home. But she hears big and heavy, PIT-A-PAT, PIT-A-PAT, comin behind her. And there's the wolf. He says, "Did you move?" in a gruff voice.

Little Daughter says, "Oh, no, dear wolf, what occasion have I to move?"

"Well, sing that sweetest, goodest song again," says the wolf.

Little Daughter sang it:

"Tray-bla, tray-bla, cum qua, kimo."

And the wolf is gone again.

The child goes back some more, *pit-a-pat, pit-a-pat, pit-a-pat,* softly on tippy-toes toward the gate.

But she soon hears very loud, PIT-A-PAT, PIT-A-PAT, comin behind

her. And there is the great big wolf, and he says to her, says, "I think you moved."

"Oh, no, dear wolf," Little Daughter tells him, "what occasion have I to move?"

So he says, "Sing that sweetest, goodest song again."

Little Daughter begins:

"*Tray-bla, tray-bla, tray-bla, cum qua, kimo.*"

The wolf is gone.

But, PIT-A-PAT, PIT-A-PAT, PIT-A-PAT, comin on behind her. There's the wolf. He says to her, says, "You moved."

She says, "Oh, no, dear wolf, what occasion have I to move?"

"Sing that sweetest, goodest song again," says the big, bad wolf.

She sang:

"*Tray bla-tray, tray bla-tray, tray-bla-cum qua, kimo.*"

The wolf is gone again.

And she, Little Daughter, *pit-a-pat, pit-a-pat, pit-a-pat*tin away home. She is so close to the gate now. And this time she hears PIT-A-PAT, PIT-A-PAT, PIT-A-PAT comin on *quick* behind her.

Little Daughter slips inside the gate. She shuts it—CRACK! PLICK!—right in that big, bad wolf's face.

She sweetest, goodest safe!

Fanciful tales such as this one often involve a curious relationship between people and animals. "A Wolf and Little Daughter" can be thought of as a wonder tale with a dreamlike quality expressed through the repetition of some of the words. The child-and-animal combination goes back to times when the slave was made the storyteller to the slaveowner's children. In these tales African sayings, words, or patter phrases survive. However, the meaning of the words does not survive in the song fragment Little Daughter sings to the wolf.

Manuel Had a Riddle

There was a king had a daughter. And the king told his kingdom that he would give a fortune in gold to anyone who could guess the riddle of the princess. But if the guesser guessed wrong, the princess would have his head cut off.

In the kingdom there was a woman who had a smart son. His name was Manuel. She was a widow and they were very poor. Manuel told his mother that he was going to the palace to try to guess the riddle of the princess and get them a fortune. Even better, he said, he would try to give the princess a riddle to guess first.

His mother begged him not to. "Manuel, do not go!" she pleaded with him. "Twenty-five men have died because they could not guess the riddle of the princess. Nobody escapes."

Manuel said, "Mother, I'm going, dead or alive. And I will escape."

His mother made him three loaves of bread and three cakes for him on his journey. She put poison in the cakes. She told him that the cakes were for him and the bread for his donkey. His donkey's name was Paul.

After they had traveled all the morning, Manuel felt hungry. He got off his donkey and he found the bread and the cakes in his bag. The bread was hard, and the cakes were soft.

"Paul has carried me so well," he said to himself, "I will give him the soft cakes and eat the hard bread myself."

When Paul ate the cakes, he fell down dead. Manuel said, "My poor little donkey is dead!"

But Manuel had to go on. And after he had gone a few steps, he saw three vultures fly down onto the donkey. They pulled out his entrails. As soon as they were eating, all three fell over dead.

Manuel went back to his dead donkey. He got the birds and tied them together, stringing them over his shoulder. He went along and he passed seven robbers.

"Will you sell us your vultures?" they asked him.

"One half-dollar apiece," Manuel said. And that's what the robbers gave him.

Manuel waited to see what the robbers were going to do with the birds. They plucked the birds; then they built a fire and cooked them. They all sat down to eat, and as soon as they began eating, they dropped down dead.

"Oh, now I have a riddle for the princess," Manuel said. And he said the riddle out loud:

> *"The cake kills Paul,*
> *Paul kills three,*
> *And three kill seven.*

"The princess will never guess my riddle," said Manuel.

Manuel arrived at the palace. He was so friendly, the nobles laughed at him. He told everybody he had come to ask the princess a riddle.

The king asked him, "Do you know what you are doing, young man?"

Manuel said, "Oh, yes, I know. If the princess guesses my riddle, you will cut off my head. But if she does not guess it, I will get a fortune."

Then Manuel asked the princess, in the proper way of asking, "What is the thing?—

> *"The cake kills Paul,*
> *Paul kills three,*
> *And three kill seven."*

The princess sat there almost thirty minutes without telling him anything. Then she told the king that she could not guess the riddle.

The king was unwilling to lose his fortune. He told Manuel, "Young man, you still have something you must do before you receive my fortune. Here, I give you three rabbits. You must set them free in the mountains. Then, in thirty days, give them back to me. But they must be fattened up, and then you will receive my fortune."

Manuel took the three rabbits and carried them away to the mountains. He was very sad. "Oh!" he said. "If I set these rabbits free here, how will I find them again?"

Just then he saw an old witch standing near him.

"What's your trouble, young man?" she asked Manuel.

"Old woman," he said, "I wonder how I will find my rabbits again if I let them run free."

The witch gave him a whistle and told him, "Whenever you want your rabbits, blow on the whistle. And wherever they are, they will come to you."

Then she was gone as quickly as she had come.

Manuel was so happy! He built a shelter for himself and he stayed there on the mountain for fifteen days. The next day he thought he would try the whistle. He blew on it. The rabbits came jumping, hop, hop, hop.

"All right! Oh, good!" Manuel cried, and he ran his hand over their fur. He felt how sleek and fat they had become.

On the twentieth day, the king told the princess to disguise herself.

"My child," he told her, "go into the mountains and give the lad any amount of money he wants for one of the rabbits."

So she did that, and when she got to the mountains, she found Manuel.

"What are you doing here?" she asked him.

"I'm fattening my three rabbits to take to the king," said Manuel.

"What, in all these mountains?" she said. "How can you find them again?"

"I have a whistle that brings them to me," he said.

"I'd love to see it," she said.

So Manuel took out the whistle. He blew on it and the three rabbits come hopping along, fatter than they were before. One of them had a black spot on its side.

The princess said, "Sell me the spotted one."

"No, I can't," Manuel said. "I have to take it to the king."

But the princess begged him. "I'll give you this bag of money I have if you will sell the spotted one to me," she said.

"Well," said Manuel, "I won't sell it to you for money. But I will take the gold heart you have hanging around your neck for it."

So the princess had to give Manuel the gold heart for the rabbit. She put the spotted rabbit in a basket and covered it with a cloth. Then she set the basket in front of her on her horse. She said goodbye and went away.

After she had left, Manuel was sorry for the loss of one of his rabbits. He thought he would whistle for it. And as soon as he did, the rabbit came jumping back to him.

When the princess reached home, she told the king and queen what must have happened to the spotted rabbit.

"You don't know very much," the queen said to her. "This time I will go get the rabbit."

So the queen went out into the mountains, where she found Manuel.

Manuel said to himself, "First came the daughter and now comes the queen. I will fix her, too!"

The queen said to Manuel, "Young man, what are you doing in this place?"

"Oh, I am fattening three rabbits to take to the king in just eight days."

"You are trying to fatten rabbits out here?" said the queen. "How can you fatten them when you can't even see them?"

"Well, I can see them whenever I wish," said Manuel.

"Oh, let me see you, then," said the queen.

So Manuel blew on the whistle and three fat rabbits came hop, hop, hopping.

"Sell me the one with the black spot," the queen commanded. "I have enough money in this bag to make you rich for your whole life."

"No," said Manuel, "I cannot sell it for money. But I'll give you the spotted rabbit in exchange for the bracelet you are wearing."

"Certainly," said the queen, "but it doesn't cost anything. Now, give me the rabbit."

Manuel put the rabbit in her basket. "I'm going to use my whistle again," he told himself.

When the queen had trotted away, he blew the whistle. The rabbit jumped out of her basket and hopped back to him.

The queen arrived at the palace and the king said to her, "I thought you were wise. That young man has some of the devil inside him. This time I will go."

The king had an iron cage made to take with him. He dressed up like a poor shepherd. He found Manuel in his hut and he said, "Young man, what are you doing here?"

"I am fattening three rabbits to take to the king," Manuel said.

"Rabbits? How strange!" said the king. "I would like to see rabbits in these hot mountains!"

"Would you really like to see them?" asked Manuel. He blew his whistle. The rabbits hopped to him.

"They are healthy and fat," said the king. "Sell me the one with the black spot. I will give you any money you wish."

"No," said Manuel. "I won't sell it. But I will give it to you in exchange for the ring you have on your finger."

The ring the king was wearing had his name on it. "I will give you this ring," said the king, "but my name is on the other side of it. Don't put it on in front of anyone, because that would bring me down low before my people."

"Oh, but this is business," Manuel said. "If you give me the ring for the rabbit, I can do what I like with it."

The king gave him the ring. Manuel took the rabbit and put it in the iron cage. Then the king left. All the rest of the day, Manuel whistled for his rabbits, but only two came. "Now I will lose my head," he told himself.

In just three days, the thirty days were up. Manuel took up the two rabbits and started for the palace. He met the same old witch at the same place he met her the first time.

"The little rabbit they stole from you is disgusted at being alone," she told Manuel. "Before you reach the palace, whistle for it and it will come to you."

When Manuel was within the palace gate, he whistled and the lost rabbit jumped along and joined the others.

"He is awfully thin," Manuel said to himself, "but I will take care of him."

When he stood before the king, the king said, "Manuel, two of the rabbits are fat and healthy. What is wrong with the third one with the spot?"

"Well, three days before I came," said Manuel, "that one got very sick; it couldn't keep any food down and that made him thin."

"Manuel, I see you are a big liar," said the king. "You must fill a sack full of lies, which will complete our account."

"Then get your sack ready—I will start," said Manuel. He started, "When I was out in the mountains, the princess came to buy a rabbit."

The princess said to him, "You lie!"

"Put it in the sack!" Manuel said.

"But how do you know she was the princess?" asked the king.

"Because I have her golden heart."

"You lie!" the princess said.

"Put it in the sack!" said Manuel. "A few days later the queen came to buy a rabbit."

"You lie!" said the queen.

"Put it in the sack!" cried Manuel.

"How do you know that it was the queen?" asked the king.

"I have her bracelet," said Manuel.

"You lie!" said the queen.

"Into the sack! Into the sack!" exclaimed Manuel. "When it lacked three days of the time for me to return, the king himself came to buy one of my rabbits."

The king said, "You lie! The sack is full! Very full!"

There, you see, the king was trying to keep Manuel from telling about his ring. He succeeded. Manuel didn't tell. He got his fortune and he took it to his mother. He and his mother then had a lot of everything and ever after they lived happily.

This is a folktale from the Cape Verde Islands that depicts episodic adventure. It seems to say that facts are facts; and yet the facts can be altered by the proper outcome of a riddle. It is one of many variations on the theme of the princess who asks riddles, with the "sack of lies" motif. There are several whistle and sack-of-lies variations. Another version is the child born with a whistle in its hand. The child would go out to whistle, and all the rats in the world would come to listen. The king hears of the whistle, wants it, etc. The child must bring him several sacks of lies or be put to death.

Papa John's Tall Tale

Papa John was an old-timer and we did what he told us. Jake was his son, and after he had his dinner, Papa John told Jake to find a horse that was fastest. Jake went to the big house, asked for the horse that was fastest.

House Jim says, "Take Missus' ridin horse, that the one is fastest."

So Jake rode Missus' mare on back over to Papa John. He got there before he left, too. And he says, "Papa, here's Fastest."

"Who the mare belong to?" asked Papa John.

"Belong to Missus," Jake says.

"How you know she is Fastest?" Papa John says.

"I know she is Fastest because I'm here before I'm gone," says Jake. And it was the truth, he had got back before he'd left. Any fool could see that.

"Well," Papa John says, "take that mare and take this pumpkin seed on your back. Don't drop it—it's heavy. Carry it on over to the field. Take a shovel and make a hole a quarter mile wide and drop that pumpkin seed in."

"That all?" asked Jake.

"No," said Papa John. "You got to get out of there as fast as you can. That's why you ridin the horse that's fastest. Don't look back, just get out of there once you drop that pumpkin seed."

So Jake did what he was told. And we was all watchin. That mare run as best she knew how, which was fastest. But it wasn't good enough.

Jake said, "Git-up-and-gone, Fastest!" He looked back, what he wasn't spose to do, which slowed him down some, and saw the pumpkin seed was growin vines, and the vines was after that fastest mare.

The mare and Jake had to climb across the leaves to keep goin. And then there were pumpkins house high. The hogs was eatin inside ofum and livin in there. So Jake and the horse ridin on through. Get on back to Papa John. Real upset, Jake was, and told him what happen.

Papa John soothes him, "That's all right, that's all right. Nothin gone get you next to me here," Papa John said. "That wasn't much

of a pumpkin seed to begin with. You shoulda been around when I was a turnip grower."

"You a turnip grower, Papa?" asked Jake.

"Was one time," Papa John said. "I plowed me two acre. I got me a mountain of manure and spread it on thick. Then I put down the turnip seed."

"What happened?" Jake asked him.

"Well, all a sudden," Papa John says, "that manure was slopped up. That turnip grew so, a herd of cows would get under a turnip leaf and sleep all day. So I had to fence it. Keep all out. Took me six months to fence around that turnip, too.

"When that turnip growed up," Papa John continued, "I had to find some way to cook it. I went down there to a man could make things. I say, 'I need a pot big and high as a hill.'

"Man says, 'I can do it. Hire me some hands to help me.'

"That's what he did," Papa John says. "He hires up a hundred hands. They dug up that hill for the clay. Then they was a-moldin and castin that hill into a pot. When it was done they had them a clay pot hill high. Then the man could make things got another hundred hands to help roll that pot atop the turnip. Wasn't no use tryin to get the turnip in the pot. So that's how we had to cook it, with the fire above the pot and the turnip under it."

"Take you long?" asked Jake.

"Well, it took about a year to get it boiled through. But it cooked up real fine, that turnip did," Papa John said.

"How long ago was that?" asked Jake.

"Oh, when you was a little fellow," Papa John said. "Been years ago."

"Well, I sure woulda liked to tasted that turnip, Papa," Jake said.

"Well, you had your chance," Papa John said. "You et the last piece of it for your dinner today."

Exaggeration tales that magnify the truth outrageously are generally called Tall Tales or simply Lies. They are also known as Münchhausens, after a German baron who told exaggerated stories about his travels. And in various parts of America they have been called toasties, gallyfloppers, windies, whoppers, and long bows. They are found throughout this country and all over the world.

Tall Tales are told with enormous solemnity about huge mosquitoes, giant vegetables, incredible hunters and marksmen, and practically anything else—such as the northern mule who got in the southerner's corncrib. It was a hot day and the corn commenced to pop, for it was popcorn. And the mule froze to death on account of he thought the popcorn was snow. . . .

—Or the potato farmer who was approached by a stranger asking to buy a hundred pounds of potatoes. The potato farmer finally said, "I can't do it. It'd be wrong to cut a potato in two."

The Two Johns

There were these two. Big John and Little John. They each had a wife. Big John had two horses that were fine horses. Little John had one horse that was sick. It wasn't any good atall.

Big John said one day to Little John, "If that horse of yours whinnies all night again, I will have to kill it." The horse did and Big John did. He killed that horse of Little John's.

Little John skinned the horse and cured the hide. Then he went away. He went walking far. He got cold and he went to a house for shelter.

The woman came to the door, says, "Well, who are you?"

"I'm Little John," he said. "I'm cold—can you let me come in?"

Woman says, "No, because my husband is away." So she shuts the door on Little John. He has to stand there out in the cold.

The husband comes home, finds Little John there, shivering in the cold. The wife comes. He says to his wife, says, "Why you leavin this man outside in the cold?"

"Well, you weren't here," she tells her husband. "I couldn't let him in."

"Well, let him in now," says the husband. So the husband, with Little John wrapped in the horsehide, walk inside. They sit down at the table to eat. Little John puts the horsehide under his feet.

"I don't have nothin but tea," says the woman, "and it's gone cold."

Little John is working his feet on the hide. He is stamping the hide hard with his feet.

"What you doin there?" the man asks Little John. "Is that hide tryin to talk to you?"

Little John says, "Hide says, go to the sideboard, you'll find food."

The man got up. He went to the sideboard there. He found food within. Plenty of food.

"What else is your horsehide saying?" asked the man.

Little John says, "Says, go back, there's wine in there."

The man goes back to his sideboard and he finds the wine.

"Oh, please, sell me your horsehide," the man begged.

"Well, I'll sell it for two baskets of money," said Little John. So he

just did. Then Little John told the man to give him back the hide and he would show him something more. He got it back and pressed his foot on it. He told the man, "Go in the next room, look in the barrel, there's something there for you to see."

The man does it. He looks in the barrel and sees the Devil. He covers it up again.

Little John had started on his way.

"Come back," said the man. "Come take away the barrel and I'll give you double."

So Little John came back. He took the Devil from the barrel and he got double money for his task.

Little John went home. He sent over to Big John's for a basket to measure his money. After he had measured it, he sent the basket back. But two silver coins had somehow stuck to the basket. Big John saw them.

"What was it you were measuring in the basket?" Big John wanted to know.

"I was measuring the money I got from my horse you killed," Little John said. "I measured more than three baskets of money."

"More than three baskets of money for that sad, weak horse?" said Big John. "I could get more than four whole baskets for my two fine horses!"

Big John went home and killed his two fine horses as soon as he got there. He cut off their skins, tied them, and hoisted them on his back. Then he went off. He went to the city and he cried out all along, "I got horsehide. Raw, raw, horsehide. Who wants to buy?"

Big John could find no one to buy his raw horsehides. He went on back home. Found Little John, said, "I'm going to kill you for your lies, Little John."

"Well, you never did it right," said Little John. "You have to cure the horsehides. Then you can sell them."

"I'm going to kill your grandmother now," said Big John. And he did. He killed Little John's good grandmother. He put her in a chair and wheeled her to the store in town and left her.

Little John comes along to the store. He asks the storekeeper for a drink. He turns to his grandmother. "Grandmother, if you weren't asleep I surely would give you a drink, too."

"Well, why don't you wake her up?" says the storekeeper.

"Well, I never like to do that," says Little John.

So the storekeeper, he did it. He went up to her. He shook her. She fell off the chair.

"What have you done?" said Little John. "You've killed my grand-mother!"

"Oh, don't tell! Don't tell!" said the storekeeper. "I'll give you some money if you don't tell anyone."

So the storekeeper paid to bury Little John's grandmother. And he gave Little John two baskets of money.

Little John, he went home, asked to borrow Big John's basket to measure. Little John still didn't have his own basket. But there were two pieces of money slipped in the sides when he returned the basket to Big John.

"Where did you get some more money?" Big John asked Little John.

"I sold my grandmother for two baskets of money," Little John told him. "See how it is? Every bad thing you do to me turns out good. You killed my horse and it turned out good. You killed my grandmother and it turned out good again."

Big John went on home. He thought about killing his own grand-mother. He planned it out. "My grandmother is much fatter and bigger than Little John's. I could get six baskets of money for her."

So Big John killed his grandmother. He put her on his back, went all into the city, said, "Who wants a dead woman? Who wants a dead grandmother? I'll sell her to you for six baskets of money."

Well, the man in charge of the city heard about it. They was after Big John now. So they are chasing him all around. He dropped the body and he ran back home.

Big John went over to Little John's house. Said, "You made me kill my grandmother, Little John, and I got not one basket of money for her. Now I will have to kill you."

Big John got Little John into a sack. Wasn't hard. Big John was big and strong, and Little John was so little. He put the sack on his back and he went on.

Now Big John passed by the church and he thought, Well, I ought to go in, get a pardon for my sins and for what I'm about to do to Little John.

So Big John went on in the church. He left the sack of Little John outside.

And a herdsman comes passing by with his cows. "What you doing in that sack, Little John?" he says.

"Well, they've put me here to throw me away into the sea," says Little John. "They're doing it because I won't marry the king's daughter."

Now that wasn't the truth, but that's what Little John told him.

Little John goes on, "I sure don't know how to eat with a knife and a fork, so how can I marry the king's daughter? I'm not going to, that's all."

The herdsman, he says, "Oh, I know how to eat with a knife and a fork. I'll marry her, I'll marry the king's daughter."

"Well, get in the sack," says Little John. And the herdsman like a fool gets in while Little John gets out.

Little John took over everything that herdsman had. Took his cows and his coat, too. And Little John took them home.

Big John come on out of the church. He picked up the sack, found it wasn't so heavy. Said, "This sack is lighter because I been pardoned of my sins."

Big John went out there to the water. He found his boat and he loaded the sack in. He went out to sea and dumped the sack.

Big John come back and went home. He saw Little John passing along with his cows, wearing a new coat.

"See, that's how it is," Little John told him. "Everything bad you do to me turns around and comes back good. You killed my horse, it turned to good. You killed my grandmother, that turned out good, too. You put me in a sack and threw me away into the sea. It was way below the water that I found these many cows and this coat."

"Well, I was so wrong," Big John said. "So put me in a sack and throw me to the sea. Throw me as far and as deep as you can, so I can get more coats and more cows."

So Little John put Big John in a sack and took him way out on the

sea. Each time Little John stopped to throw the sack of Big John into the water, Big John would say, "No, go farther, Little John. Go farther." Big John said that three times, and three times Little John had to go farther out on the water.

At last he was far enough. "This is it. This is the place," said Big John. "Throw me out."

So Little John threw Big John way out, deep in the sea. And then Little John rowed back to shore. He got out, took up the empty sack, and went home.

He had a good life and it was peaceful.

This is a black Portuguese tale of grisly realism with variants in Spanish and English from Louisiana, Puerto Rico, the Bahamas, and the Philippines. It is at once a comic and an outrageously gruesome tale. And it is cousin to the Foolish John and Wise John tales (Jeane Sotte and John Esprit) from Louisiana, where the little man is smart and the big man foolish.

Wiley, His Mama, and the Hairy Man

Now, facts are facts. Wiley was a boy. He and his mama lived by themselves with just Wiley's dogs. Say Wiley's papa fell off the ferry boat one time. The river was quick there where he fell. They looked for Wiley's papa a long way down the river and in the pools of the sandbanks. And say they never found him. But they heard a great bad laughin way off across the river. And everybody sayin it, "That's the Hairy Man." Sayin Wiley's papa never got across Jordan because the Hairy Man block his way.

"Wiley," his mama tell him, "the Hairy Man's got your papa and he's gone get you if you don't look out."

"Yes, Mama," Wiley said. "I'll look out. I'll take my hound dogs everywhere I go. You know, the Hairy Man can't stand some hound dogs."

Wiley knew this because his mama had told him. She knew because she was from the swamps near the Tombigbee River and she knew *conjure*. Knew how to lay tricks, put together charms, or take the tricks away. She could find a vein of water. She could see in front of her and behind her, and so was called a "two-head." So she knew.

One day Wiley taken up his axe and went in the swamp to cut him some poles for a hen roost. He took his hound dogs with him. The dogs went off, runnin after a wild pig. That thing run so far off, Wiley couldn't hear his hounds atall.

"Well, I hope the Hairy Man is somewhere away and nowhere around here," Wiley said.

He picked up his axe to start work. But before he could begin, he spied the Hairy Man through the trees. Hairy Man just grinnin at him. Hairy Man was ugly, even when he grinned. He was coarse-hairy all over. His eyes burned red as fire. He had great big teeth, with spit all in his mouth and runnin down his chin. He was a terrible-lookin Hairy Man.

"Don't you look at me like that," Wiley said. "Don't you come near me." But the Hairy Man kept on comin and grinnin.

Wiley threw down his axe and scrambled up a big laurel tree. He sees the Hairy Man hasn't any feet like a man. He has hooves like a cow's. And Wiley had never seen a cow way up a laurel tree. So he knew he was safe. He climbed almost to the top. He looked down. Then he did climb to the top.

"Why come you climbin up that tree?" asked the Hairy Man.

"My mama tole me to stay away from you, Hairy Man. But what you got there in your croaker sack?"*

"Haven't got nothin, yet," said the Hairy Man.

"Go on away from here," said Wiley.

"Ha! I will not!" said the Hairy Man. He picked up Wiley's axe. He swung it like a strong man. And the wood chips flew out of that tree.

Wiley grabbed the tree as tight as he could. He rubbed his belly up against the tree trunk. And he hollered, "Fly, wood chips, fly! Go back in your same old place!" He meant for the wood chips to go back into the tree trunk.

And the chips flew back. And that Hairy Man fumed, stomped, and was fit to be tied. Then he swung the axe again. And Wiley knew he must holler faster. So the two of them went to it, tooth and toenail. Wiley was hollerin and that Hairy Man was choppin. Wiley hollered till he was hoarse; and pity, he saw that the Hairy Man was gaining on him.

"I'll come down partway if you'll make this tree twice as big around," Wiley said.

"I'm not studyin you," said the Hairy Man. He swung the axe and swung the axe.

"I bet you can't do it," said Wiley. "I bet you can't make it bigger."

"I won't even try," said the Hairy Man.

* A sack in which to keep animals that make croaking sounds, such as frogs.

So they went back to it again. With Wiley a-hollerin and the Hairy Man just choppin away. Wiley about yelled himself finished when he thought of somethin his mama had told him. She had said, "Tell the Hairy Man you goin to pray, and then call your dogs."

Wiley yelled to the Hairy Man, "Stop it now. I got to pray!"

"What's that mean?" asked the Hairy Man.

"Means I got to pray to the Man Above," said Wiley.

The Hairy Man knew what that meant, although he'd never heard prayer, and he stayed quiet a moment while Wiley chanced to pretend to pray.

"Heah-aaah, dogs! Heah-aaah!" Wiley hollered. "Fly, wood chips, fly! Go back in your same old place!"

"You got no dogs," the Hairy Man said. "I sent that wild pig to draw them off."

"I'm just still prayin," Wiley said, and hollered again, "Heah-aaah, dogs!" They both heard the hound dogs comin on strong, yelpin in a close pack.

The Hairy Man looked worried. "Come on down," he said, "and I'll teach you how to *conjure.*"

"I can learn all the *conjure* I need from my mama," said Wiley, and he could, too.

The Hairy Man fumed and muttered. But he threw down the axe and hightailed it off through the swamp.

Well, when Wiley got himself home, safe, he told his mama that the Hairy Man had almost got him that time. Hairy Man would have, too, but that he pretended to pray and called his hounds instead and the hounds run the Hairy Man off.

"Did he have his sack?" his mama asked Wiley.

"Yesum," Wiley said.

"Next time he come after you, don't you climb some tree," said his mama.

"I won't," said Wiley, "cause some tree not big enough around."

"Don't climb atall. Just stay on the ground and say, 'Hello, Hairy Man.' You hear me, Wiley?" asked his mama.

"Nosum."

"He won't hurt you, Wiley," his mama said. "You can put that Hairy Man down on the ground in the dirt, once I tell you how to do him."

"But if I put him in the dirt, he'll put me in the croaker sack," said Wiley.

"You just do what I say. You say, 'Hello, Hairy Man,' " his mama said. "And he says, 'Hello, Wiley.' And you say, 'Hairy Man, I heard you the best *conjure* doctor around here.' And he say, 'I reckon I am.' And you say, 'I bet you can't turn yourself into a giraffe.' You keep tellin him he can't, Wiley," his mama told him, "and then he is sure to turn himself into a giraffe. Then you say, 'I bet you can't turn yourself into an alligator.' And he will, too. Then you say, 'Anybody can turn theyselves into somethin big as a man. But I bet you can't turn yourself into a possum.' And the Hairy Man will, and you grab him and throw him in the croaker sack."

"Well," said Wiley, "it don't sound just right somehow, but I'll try it." So he tied up the dogs so they wouldn't scare away the Hairy Man. And he went down to the swamp again. Wiley hadn't been there long when he looked up, and here come the Hairy Man. Just grinnin through the trees. Just as hairy all over and big teeth showin so wet. He could tell Wiley was out there without his hound dogs. Wiley nearly climbed a tree when he saw that croaker sack. But he didn't. "Hello, Hairy Man," he said.

"Hello, Wiley," said the Hairy Man. He took the sack off his shoulder and started openin it up.

"Hairy Man, I heard you were the best *conjure* doctor around these parts," Wiley said.

"I reckon that's true," said the Hairy Man.

"I bet you can't turn yourself into a giraffe," Wiley said.

"Shoot, that's no trouble atall," said the Hairy Man.

"I bet you can't do it," Wiley said.

So the Hairy Man twisted, made a long neck; and twisted around, made him long legs, and turned himself into a giraffe.

"Well, I bet you can't turn yourself into an alligator," Wiley said.

The giraffe twisted, got short legs and twisted around, got him thick skin, and turned into an alligator. He was watchin Wiley to see he didn't try to run.

"Anybody can turn theyselves into somethin big as a man," said Wiley, "but I bet you can't turn yourself into a possum."

The alligator twisted, got smaller and twisted around, long tail, and turned himself into a possum.

Just quick! Wiley grabbed it and threw it in the sack. He tied the

sack up good and tight, and then he threw it in the river. Wiley went home through the swamp. He looked up, and there came the Hairy Man grinnin through the trees.

"I turned myself into the wind and blew out of there," said the Hairy Man. "Wiley, I'm gone set right here till you get hungry and fall out of that tree you up in again. You want me to teach you some more *conjure?*"

Wiley thought awhile. He pondered over the Hairy Man and he worried about his hound dogs tied up a mile away.

"Well," Wiley said, "you sure lay some pretty good tricks. But I bet you can't make things disappear and go who knows where."

"Huh, that's what I'm good at," said the Hairy Man. "Look at that old bird nest on the limb there. Now look again! It's gone for good and true."

"Now how I know it was there in the first place?" asked Wiley. "I didn't see it in the first place, either, let alone seein it gone. But I bet you can't make somethin I know is there disappear."

"Ha, ha," laughed the Hairy Man. "Look at your shirt."

Wiley looked down and his shirt was gone. But he didn't care. It was what he wanted the Hairy Man to do.

"That was just a plain old shirt," Wiley said. "But this rope I got tied round my pants has got my mama's *conjure* on it. I bet you can't make *it* disappear."

"Huh, I can make all the rope in this county disappear," the Hairy Man said.

"Ha ha ha," said Wiley.

The Hairy Man looked mad and threw his chest way out. He opened his mouth wide and hollered loud. "From now on, all the rope in this county has gone and disappeared!"

And truly, the belt that had held up Wiley's pants was gone. And quick! Wiley reared back holdin his pants up with one hand and onto a tree limb with the other. "Heah-aaah, dogs!" he hollered, loud enough to be heard two miles away. The rope that had tied up his dogs was gone, too. And the dogs came and the Hairy Man lit out through the swamp one more time.

Well, then, when Wiley and his dogs got back to home, his mama asked him did he put the Hairy Man in the sack.

"Yesum, but he turned himself into the wind and blew right on out of that old croaker sack."

"That's too bad," said his mama. "But you fooled him twice. If you fool him again, he'll leave you alone. But he'll be mighty hard to fool the third time."

"We have to think hard on how to fool him," Wiley said.

"I'll work on it directly," said his mama. She sat down by the fire with her chin in her hands. Wiley was just there, worryin about keepin the Hairy Man away from him. He took his dogs out and tied one at the back door and one at the front door. He crossed a broom and an axe handle over the window. He built a fire in the fireplace. Wiley felt a lot safer. Then he sat down next to his mama to help her think hard. After a while, she said, "Wiley, go down to the pen and get that little baby pig away from the sow."

Wiley did as he was told. He took the squealin pig out of the pen and back to his mama. She put the little pig in his bed.

"Now, Wiley," she said, "go clear up in the hayloft and hide."

So Wiley did as he was told again. And before long, he heard the wind howlin and the trees blowin and shakin. The dogs started growlin. He could see through a knothole. And the dog at the front door was starin down at the swamps. Its hair standin up and its lips drawn back in a snarl, too. Then an animal as big as a mule with horns on its head ran out of the swamp past the house. The dog jumped and jumped but he couldn't get loose.

A great big animal, like a giant dog with a long snout, came runnin out of the swamp and snarled at the cabin. And this time one dog broke loose and took out after the big animal, and the animal headed back to the swamp.

Wiley looked out again in time to see his other dog break loose. The dog took out after another funny-lookin animal.

"Oh, my goodness," Wiley moaned. "I just know the Hairy Man is comin after me!"

And it was true, because in no time Wiley heard somethin with big hooves clompin like a cow up on the roof. He heard somethin swear to heaven when it touched the hot chimney.

The Hairy Man saw that there was a fire in the fireplace. So he came off that roof and dared to come up and knock on the front door.

"Miz Mama," he hollered, "I've come to get your baby boy, Wiley."

"You won't get my baby," Wiley's mama hollered right back.

"Give him over. If you don't, I'll sure bite you and poison you."

"I'll bite you right back," Wiley's mama said.

"Give him here or I'll set your house afire with my lightnin," the Hairy Man said.

"Well, I do have my sweet cream to put it out with," Wiley's mama said.

The Hairy Man heaved against the door and said, "Give him over to me if you don't want me to dry up your spring, make your cow come sick, and send a field of boll weevils out of the ground. They'll eat every cotton boll you've got."

"Hairy Man," said Wiley's mama, "you wouldn't do that. That's too mean, even for you."

"Oh, I'm mighty mean," said the Hairy Man. "I'm the meanest man I ever did see."

"Well, if I give over my baby, will you go on away and leave all else here alone?" asked Wiley's mama.

"That is just what I'll do," the Hairy Man said.

And with that, Wiley's mama opened the door and let in the Hairy Man.

"The baby's just there, in the bed," Wiley's mama said.

The Hairy Man came in, lookin meaner than anythin. He went over to the bed, pulled the covers off.

He hollered, "There's nothin here but a sucklin pig!"

"Well," said the mama, "I never said what *kind* of baby I was givin up. And that little pig did belong to me before I gave it over to you, Mister Hairy Man."

"Shoot!" hollered the Hairy Man. He raged and he yelled. He stomped and yammered and bared his drippin teeth. Finally, he took the pig and tore out to the swamp. He knocked down trees and let loose rocks and boulders all the way. In the mornin, say there was a big, wide path right through the swamp just like a cyclone cut along through it. Trees torn clear up, roots and all, and lyin there on the ground.

After all that, when it was most safe, Wiley came down from the loft.

"Is that man gone, Mama?" he asked his good mama.

"Oh, yes, child," said his mama. "Old Hairy Man won't hurt you ever again. Because we did surely fool him three times."

And that was the end of that. But they say that Hairy Man is still deep in the swamps somewhere. Say he is waitin on the right time.

In this exaggerated-reality tale, in which facts are altered by the use of magic powers and charms, the weak triumph over the strong. The weak are again wise, but with the added benefit of "conjuration." There is the added motif of "the villain overcome by the hero's dogs." Another version of the Hairy Man tale has a "widder woman" being caught in the woods by old Hairy. The "fooling the 'ogre' three times" motif appears in this story as a favorable conjuring trick.

A conjurer is a witch doctor, a medicine man or woman, hoodoo doctor, root doctor, or voodoo priestess who knows how to work magic through the use of a charm. Most of the charms are of African origin.

JOHN AND THE DEVIL'S DAUGHTER

And Other Tales of the Supernatural

John and the Devil's Daughter

Let's talk about one time. This young man, John who could conquer. They call him John de Conquer. He's goin out huntin for a labor. But he is huntin the Devil. He expects to get some work with him. But there is no wagon ride to there. You have to find the witch lady. So he did, he found her. She had this giant bird. Call him a great big kinda eagle.

"How much it cost to ride?" John de Conquer asked the witch lady.

"Cost you meat," she told him.

"How much meat?" he says.

And she says, "Beef in quarters. Mebbe three quarters beef."

"That much?" he says.

And she says, "When my giant eagle lets a screechin, you give him a quarter beef."

So he did, John got on, paid the meat. And the eagle took off, risin, flappin his wings. John held on to the biggest feather he could reach. Big as a pine tree, it was. Eagle just flew and flew. Ten mile. One hundred. One thousand miles. That eagle let out a screechin.

And John de Conquer takes up his sack of beef. He gets a quarter. Tosses it to the eagle. Eagle catches it in his beak.

Another thousand miles. Eagle lets out a mighty noise, as big as a cloud.

John gets the sack, gives him another quarter beef.

Eagle is full up. He flies and flies maybe two thousand miles now. And then he comes swoopin low. And then he lands. John de Conquer hangin from a pinfeather and then lettin go. He is down on the ground.

She is standin right there—the Devil's daughter.

John says to her, "I'm huntin some work with the Devil. Have you seen him?" He's not a bit scared of her.

"Oh well," she says, "the Devil is my daddy. He'll give you a labor, but don't you take it. Others have come for work and he has killed them."

John asks, "Well, why?"

And the Devil's daughter tells him, says, "Because none of them could do it. They couldn't do the work he give them."

"Is that so?" says John. Says, "Well, I have to find some work."

"Well," she says, "if you have to, then. You just do what he says, just try to do it."

"Will you help me out?" asks John. He was seein how pretty she was.

"I will help you," she said, and smiled at him. She saw he was some handsome.

So she taken him to her father. Says to the Devil, says, "Daddy, I brought this one to meet you. Name of John. Lookin for a labor."

Devil says to big John, "All right. Here's some work. First thing in the mornin, you clear me some land. Some sixty acres. Don't take all day. Just half a day. Make sure the trees is cut. Don't leave 'em."

So big John de Conquer is up and out the next day without any breakfast. It's way early. He wants to get a head start. He cuts one or two big trees by ten o'clock. He's got acres to go.

The Devil's daughter comes out there right by where he's workin. She feels sorry for him. He's way behind. He'll never make two days, let alone half a day.

She says, "Gimme that hatchet."

He does and she shows him a thing or two. Talkin to the hatchet, says to the hatchet, "Let one tree fall, all will fall. Trim one limb, trim all. Burn one branch, burn all."

The sixty acres is cut, on fire, and burned up in a second. Nothin is left to bother the eye smoothin its lookin over the land.

Then the daughter goes off. The Devil comes out to see what John de Conquer has done. "Did you do my work the way I said?" Devil asks him.

"It got done," John de Conquer says. That wasn't a lie.

Devil nods. "Not bad. Pretty good," he says. "Now, in the mornin, you go plow that sixty acres. You go plant it. I want some roastin ears good and sweet for my meal tomorra night."

John gets up way early in the mornin. He hitches the horses and plows up straight rows. But it's after eleven and he hasn't plowed ten acres yet.

Devil's daughter is there. Brings John a jug of water for his thirst. He drinks all of it, he was that thirsty. She says to him, "I'll plow it for you." She's got her eye on him. Stuck on him.

She talks to the plow, says, "Plow one row, plow all. Plant a kernel, plant all. Corn, grow high over my head.

"Now," she says to John, "pick yourself some good corn ears for my Devil daddy."

So he does.

Now the daughter knows the father is going to kill John anyhow. Cause John de Conquer is just too big for him. But John don't know nothin.

"We could get married," she tells John.

"The Devil will kill us both," John tells her.

"Well, I got me two fastest horses. We'll go get them," the daughter says. "When Daddy's asleep, we'll just ride off. Then we'll marry."

So that was the plan. Waitin until the Devil is asleep.

Midnight. They go out for the horses that belong to the Devil. They get on and ride off. Daughter says, "Horses run on, run on, five hundred mile. Jump it."

When it's mornin, they are way far away from there. But so is the

Devil. He waked up, see, when they went out. Seen his daughter taken his favorite horses. And he has on his boots hip high. John and the Devil's daughter look back and the Devil is sayin to the boots: "Step it, I say, high step it. Make each step five hundred mile."

So the Devil daddy is almost to them. And daughter don't know what to do.

John de Conquer says, "Don't know what to do, but we better hurry up and move."

"Well, I thought of somethin now," she says. "You be a fox," she says to John. She turns herself into a pond of water with a duck on it swimmin.

And so John de Conquer, big as anythin, is an old, gray fox.

The fox is tryin to get at the duck when the Devil high-steps by. Devil can't see it's them. Just sees a gray fox tryin to snap up a duck on the pond.

The Devil, he went on. But his legs are worn out. His feet hurt him. And his boots are steamin. He has to get a big old animal, looks like a great big bull.

"Come on," says the daughter to John. "He's gone back for his bull. We'll make some time up." So they hurried along. "Jump, five hundred," girl says to the horses. "Jump a thousand, five hundred." And so the horses did.

Half a day later she looks back. Who's comin?

That's who. Devil comin on, sayin, "You bull, you bull, jump it."

She says, "My daddy is comin with his bull under him. He's ridin hard."

John tells her, "I don't know what to do about your Devil daddy."

So they were passin some thorny bushes and she tells him, "Reach me some thorns."

So John does it. He hands a whole thorny bush over to her.

She takes it from him and she says, "Plant one thorn, plant all. Up thorns, four feet up, ten feet up, fifteen. Ten, no, fifteen feet wide. Make it a thousand, five hundred miles long."

That thorn hedge went on long about forever.

The Devil comin up to the thorn hedge, ridin the biggest, reddest fire bull in the Hell world. The bull couldn't get through the thorns.

Devil says, says, "I'll go back and get my hatchet. I bet I'll get through then." So he went back.

And he come back. And it took him hot summers and cold winters to cut through that what his daughter had built up. The thorn hedge. And by then there wasn't a scent of nothin. No horses. No daughter. No big John de Conquer.

But they say John and the Devil's daughter made it all right. The Devil never caught them. They got married. Say they farmed all around and John and her made a good home. Had lots of children. Lived happily forever after.

That's all.

Attempts to control the environment, people, or situations brought the concept of witches to the black folktale. "John and the Devil's Daughter" is a Märchen, a tale of the supernatural and magic in which the Devil plays a main part. John must visit the "witch lady" in order to get work. Extraordinary powers out of darkness—the witch's giant eagle—give an added dimension as an aid to the hero in getting his way. The Devil's daughter also has power, and by marrying her, John de Conquer, the legendary black hero, adds her strength to his. De Conquer, the little-known mythical hero, is said to have come to America from Africa on a slave ship following the wind like an albatross.

Variants of this tale appear worldwide, with the motif of "the girl as helper in the hero's flight" being most popular in the American South and in the West Indies. There are Jack tale versions in which the hero is always known as Jack. There are also Amerindian versions. Often in the black versions the hero is simply called John. "Help from the ogre's daughter" and "obstacle flight" motifs are quite common.

The Peculiar Such Thing

A long time ago way off in the high piney woods lived a fellow all alone. He lived in a one-room log cabin. There was a big old fireplace, and that is where this fellow cooked his supper to eat it right in front of the fire.

One night, after the fellow had cooked and ate his supper, somethin crept through the cracks of the cabin logs. That somethin was the most peculiar such thing the fellow ever saw. And it had a *great, big, long tail.*

As soon as the fellow saw that somethin with its *great, big, long tail,* he reached for his axe. With a swoopin strike with it, he cut the somethin's tail clean off. The peculiar such thing crept away through the cracks between the logs, and was gone.

This fellow, like he had no sense, he cooked the *great, big, long tail.* Yes, he did. It tasted sweet and he ate it. Goodness! And then he went to bed, and in a little while he went off to sleep.

The fellow hadn't been asleep very long before he woke right up again. He heard somethin climbin up the side of his cabin. It sounded mighty like a cat. He could hear it scratchin and tearin away. And pretty soon he heard it say, *"Tailypo, tailypo. Give me back my tailypo."*

Now the fellow livin there all alone did have some dogs. Big one was Best and the other two slight ones was All Right and Fair. And when that fellow heard somethin, he called his dogs, "Yuh! Dawgs! Come on!" like that. And his dogs come flyin out from under the cabin. And they chased the peculiar such thing away down a far piece. Then this fellow went on back to bed. He went to sleep.

It was deep in the middle of the next night when the fellow woke up. He heard somethin by his front door tryin to get in. He listened hard and he could hear it scratchin and tearin away. And he heard it say, *"Tailypo, tailypo. Give me back my tailypo."*

Fellow sat up in his bed. He called his dogs, "Yuh! You, Best, you All Right, you Fair, come on in!" like that. And the dogs busted around the corner. And they caught up with the peculiar such thing at the gate, and they about broke they own tails tryin to catch it. This time they chased what it was down into the big hollow there.

And the fellow, well, he went back to bed and went to sleep.

It was way long toward mornin, the fellow woke up and he hears somethin down in the big swamp. He had to listen. He heard it say, *"You know you got it. I know you know. Give me back my tailypo."*

That man sat up in bed. He called his dogs, "You the Best, you All Right, and you Fair. Yuh! Come on in here!"

Well, this time, the dogs never come. The thing down there in the hollow musta carried them off in there. It musta eaten the first one, says, *"That's best."* It eaten the other two, says, *"That ain't but all right and fair."*

And the fellow went back to bed. Don't see how he could sleep again. But he didn't know how bad off his dogs was by then.

Well, it was just daybreak. The fellow was awake. Scared, he didn't know why. Musta heard somethin. Somethin right there with him in the room. It sounded like a cat climbin up the covers at the foot of his bed. He listened. He could hear it, scratchin and tearin away.

The fellow look at the foot of his bed. He's seein two little pointy ears comin up over the edge of the bed. In another minute, he's seein two big, scary-red eyeballs lookin straight at him. He can't say nothin. He can't scream, he's too scared to death.

That peculiar such thing at the foot of the bed kept on creepin up, creepin up. By and by, it was right on top of the fellow. And it said in his face in a real low voice, *"Tailypo, tailypo. Give me back my tailypo."*

That man loses his voice, loses his power of speech. But finally, he can say it. Says, "I hasn't got it. I hasn't got your tailypo!"

And that somethin that was there, that peculiar such thing, says right back, *"Yes you has!"* It jumped on that fellow and it was fierce. Its big teeth tore at him, made him ribbons. They say it got its tailypo back.

Fellow's cabin fall to ruin. It rot. It crumble and it disappear. Nothin left to it in the big woods but the place where it was.

And the folks that live near that place say that deep in the night, when the moon is goin down and the wind blows across the place just right, you can hear some peculiar such thing callin, *"Tailypo, tailypo . . ."* like that. And then, the sound of it do just fade away with the moonlight. Like it never even ever was.

A tale told in moderate dialect, "The Peculiar Such Thing" is considered by some to be a fairy tale that can be traced to English fairy tales. The tale teller had fun with ghosts and didn't take them too seriously. However, this black American version has a fright or horror tactic to it that gives more of the feeling of a ghost tale, with the "thing" returning for its missing part. The repetition of *"Tailypo, tailypo. Give me back my tailypo"* depends upon the teller's voice for its frightening effect.

Little Eight John

Little Eight John come be a small boy, say he lived long ago. He was a handsome one. But lookin good never fit to the way he acted. Little Eight John was mean, some. He never paid much attention to the older folks, nor listened to the truth they knew about. His mama loved him ever so much. She'd tell him not to do somethin and Little Eight John would go right ahead and do somethin awful. That was the way he was. Awful contrary.

"Eight John," his mama sayin, "now don't you go steppin on no toads and frogs. Toads and frogs is bad luck. If you bother with them, you'll bring bad luck on the family."

Little Eight John says, "Mama, I won't step on the toad-frogs. I won't step on them!"

But once out of sight of his good mama, Little Eight John went right ahead on and found him a toad and a frog. And he squished the toad. Then he squashed the frog. And if he could find them, he'd squish up and squash up a whole bucket of toad-frogs.

His mama's cow wouldn't give the good milk one time. His baby sister had bad stomachaches. Little Eight John just laughed and laughed about it.

"Honey, don't sit in that chair backwards," his mama told him one time. "You sittin down in every chair backwards and you gone bring real serious bad to your family."

Of course, Little Eight John just sittin down backwards in every chair he could find anywhere.

One day his mama's corn bread burned up with her lookin at it rise. The milk wouldn't churn no single way at all that she tried it.

Little boy Eight John fell to laughin and laughin so, because he knew why things happen to be the way they bein.

"Sweet Little Eight," his mama told him, "don't you climb a tree on a Sunday, or it will be bad luck."

So bad Little Eight John, he such an awful little boy, he went around sneakin around and climbin trees on a Sunday.

It happened soon that his papa's potaters would not grow. His papa's mule would not plow. Little Eight John surely knew why that was, but he wasn't tellin a soul.

"Don't count your straight, white teeth," his mama told Little

Eight John, "else there will come an awful sickness to your family."

But angry Little Eight John, he went right ahead and counted his teeth in his mouth. Counted the uppers; counted the lowers. He counted them on Mondays and Sundays and the days in between. Until he had counted them all eighty hundred times, that child.

Then his poor mama had the whooping cough and the little baby had what was the croup sickness. All because Little Eight John was so terrible, he brought trouble to his family.

His sweet mama told him straight, "Little Eight John," she said, "don't go sleepin with your head at the foot of the bed. It will give your family the short-of-money blues, if you do."

He did it. Little Eight John did sleep with his head at the foot of the bed because he was such a rotten little child.

His family went stone broke with no money nowhere hidden. And that made Little Eight John giggle and grin.

"Don't you dare give yourself Sunday moans, for fear of Old Raw Head Bloody Bones," his mama told him because she loved him so.

Now Little Eight John knew that the Old Bloody Bones was the raw bones of someone dead that could rise and walk and try to catch somebody. But Little Eight John, he didn't care one bit. He moaned and he groaned on a Sunday and a Monday, too. He was just so contrary.

And sure enough, one dark, still night, it happened. Old Raw Head Bloody Bones rose up and came walkin. He come after bad Little Eight John. And in one flicker of candlelight, that Old Raw Head Bloody Bones turned Little John into a little dark spot. There was that dark spot like a grease spot on the kitchen table.

The next morning, Little Eight John's mama taken a wet rag and wash off that grease-lookin spot on the kitchen table. "Musta missed the grease there last supper," she said. She rubbed and rubbed at it until the dark spot was all gone. Wasn't not a streak of it left.

And that was the end of Little Eight John.

What happens to all little chil'ren who never mind.

This is a moral tale told particularly to children so they will be good! At other times, it was meant to be told as frightening entertainment. It can be placed historically with a slavery folk rhyme whispered to plantation slave children as they went to bed:

> *Don' talk—go ta sleep!*
> *Eyes shut an' don' you peep!*
> *Keep still, or he jes moans,*
> *Raw Head an' Bloody Bones!*

Jack and the Devil

One time, there was a wicked man named Jack. He treated his wife like a dog. He treated his children like dirt. He had a habit of drinkin whiskey from mornin till night. That stuff burned him up inside himself, and that was when the Devil come to get him.

Jack saw that Devil standin there. He was scared to death and he moaned and fell down. Jack begged the Devil to just let him off this time, just this time. Let him stay a little longer on the earth.

But the Devil said to him, said, "Uh-unh, Jack. I can't wait for you any longer. My wife, Abbie, is expectin you."

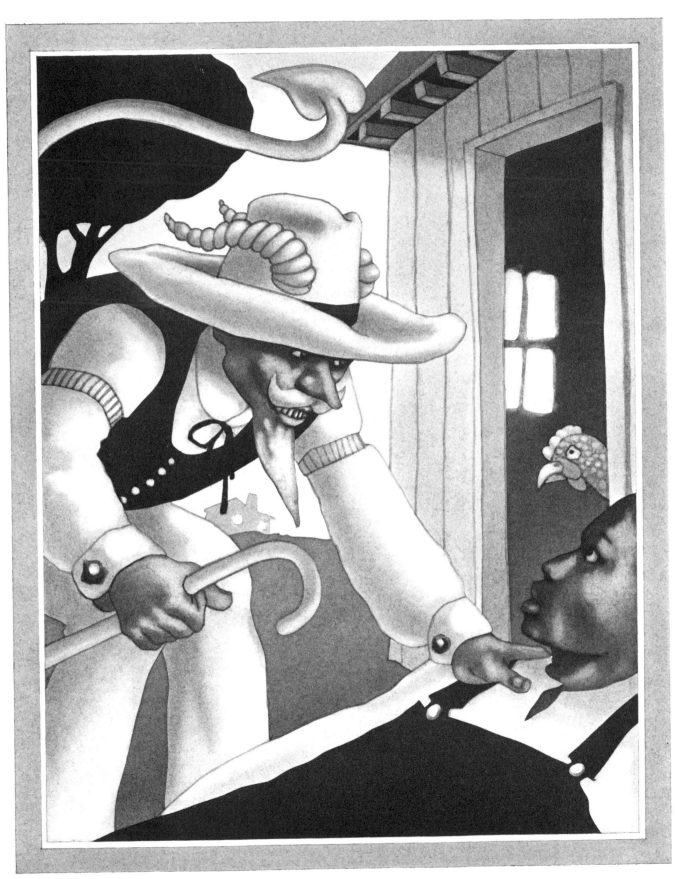

So the Devil, he starts out for his home. And Jack, he had to follow until they come upon a drinkin place.

"Mister Devil," says Jack, "do you want a drink?"

The Devil says, says, "Well, guess I do want one. But you, see, Jack, I don't have the change; we never keep no change down there at my home place."

"Well, Mister Devil," says Jack, "tell you what I'll do for you. I got ten cent in my pocket. If you'll change yourself into another ten cent, we can get two drinks. Then you can change yourself back to a Devil again."

Well, the Devil thought that was fair. He changed himself into ten cent. Jack picked him up, but he didn't go to that drinkin place. Nosir. Jack put that ten cent in his pocketbook. Pocketbook was a little change purse with a cross for its clasp. He shut that up tight and the Devil couldn't get out of it, couldn't get by that clasp in the shape of a cross.

Well, the Devil begged and cussed and carried on, but Jack paid him no mind. He went on toward home.

The Devil call to him, says, "Jack, if you let me out, I'll let you stay free for a whole year. Lemme go, please Jack, cause my wife, Abbie, is too little to keep the fires high. All will go black and cold down there if I don't hurry and see to the home place."

Jack thought about it this way. He says to himself, says, "I might let him go. Cause in a year I could repent and get my faith in the church. I could get rid of him through religion."

So Jack said, "Mister Devil, I'll let you out if you swear you won't come after me for twelve whole months."

"I promise, Jack" came the muffled voice of the Devil from inside the pocketbook.

So Jack undid the cross that was a clasp, and the Devil was gone. Jack never saw him go atall. "Now I will repent," he says to himself. "And I don't have to hurry. I got me twelve free months before the Devil can take me. The last three of them months is plenty of time to get my religion good. Where's that ten cent I had? Oh, heah it tis. I'm gone get me a drink, too."

After six long months were gone, Jack decided that the last one of the twelve months would be long enough for him to repent. He would have himself a drinkin spree, and the last ten days of the month would be just time for him to repent.

When the last week come, Jack had drunk so much, he was lyin in bed all the time, seein things that were not there. But then the Devil was right there, for it was after the last day of the year that Jack had for his freedom. And the Devil had come for him for true. And poor Jack, he had to get up and follow the Devil on out of there.

After a long time of goin, the Devil and Jack pass a tree full of big, sweet apples.

"Do you want some apples, Mister Devil?" Jack asked him.

"Well, if you want some, you can get you some," the Devil tells Jack. He stopped to look up at the tree.

"How you expect a man sick as me to climb a tree?" Jack says. "Here, you catch hold of that bough there," he told the Devil, "and I'll push you on up to the fork in the tree, and you can get all the apples."

So the Devil starts up and Jack pushes him until he is up there.

And the Devil starts to touch and squeeze at the apples to find the best ones.

Now while the Devil was busy with the apples, Jack whips his knife out and cuts a big cross right there in the bark below where the Devil is workin.

The Devil hollers out, "Ah-la! Somethin almost hit me. What you doin down there, Jack? If you messin around, I'll cut your heart out!"

But the Devil couldn't get out of the tree because the cross was there. Jack sat himself down right by the tree and listened to the Devil ragin and cussin a blue streak.

So Jack kept the Devil there all that night and into the next mornin, when the Devil says to him, says, "Jack, let me down from here and I'll give you another year."

"You gimme nothin," Jack told him, and he stretched out on the grass.

Long about sunset, the Devil says, "Jack, cut out that cross from there so I can get down, and I'll give you ten years."

"Nosir, Mister Devil," Jack says. "I won't let you down until you swear you will leave me alone forever."

Well, the Devil found out that Jack was tough, he was hard and cold as ice. So he agreed to leave Jack alone forever, too. Jack cut the cross off that apple tree and the Devil walked away without another word.

After that, Jack never thought a minute about repentin or being good or gettin religion. He wasn't afraid of the Devil at all no more. He lived a long time. But one dark day, his old body give out on him. He had to die. And he did.

He went to the gate of Heaven askin to get in. The angels there just shook their heads at him. So then Jack went off to the gate of Hell. He heard the Devil hollerin at his little imps: "Shut that gate fast as you can. Don't let that man in here! He treated me worse than awful twice times. Tell him to go on back where he come from."

Jack calls to him, "But Mister Devil, how will I find my way in the dark? Will you gimme a lantern?"

"Well, here, then," the Devil say. And he take a chunk of red-hot burnin coals out of his fire. "Take this on with you, Jack," he says, "and don't you ever come back here no more, too."

Jack, he took the fire. But he got himself lost. They say he is still wanderin in the dark. Some say you can see his little light a-bobbin this-away and that-away when the night is coldest and the chill is deepest.

This tale is one of many Devil tales about individuals who associate with the Devil for personal gain or pleasure, only to end up worse off than when they started. In the end Jack is too much for even the Devil. He is not wanted in Heaven or Hell, and he must wander the earth with his little light. But of course, he is dead, and the little light, often called "will-o'-the-wisp," represents the light of his soul. Stories of marsh light or will-o'-the-wisp light are many and varied.

Better Wait Till Martin Comes

Now here's a story I heard tell. About John. And he was a man travelin through one end this county to the other. One time, he gets caught after dark. Had no place to stay nearby. There was a tumble-down plantation house on the hill, next to a lone pine tree. Real old, abandoned mansion. Both house and tree were twisted. Seemed to John he'd heard the place was haunted.

John didn't worry much about haunts. He knew himself to be a good man, and he knew his prayers.

Expect I better take shelter up there in the big house, he thought.

The sky do look cloudy. Think it might rain before mornin.

So John walked over the weedy ground past the tree. He heard that skinny pine moan. Then it meowed at him.

John looked straight ahead. If there were haunts in the tree, they wasn't goin to catch him lookin. He went ahead on inside the old plantation house. All old houses like that whisper. Empty rooms. And this moaned, as well. Wind through the cracks. John paid no mind to the forlorn sounds. He found plenty of dry wood on the hearth next to the fireplace. And soon he had a cracking, warm fire goin, too.

"That's the best fire I ever made, if I do say so myself." He spoke out loud to keep himself company.

John found a broken-down chair. It would hold his weight a minute, so he sat down in it. And after a time he was most comfortable there in the empty, whisperin, moanin plantation house. He was safe against any storm. He folded his hands. And he said his prayers over to himself for good measure.

Shortly, somethin come up behind John. Then it walked on by him. It was a black, shiny cat, walkin in out of the rain. It was blacker than night and blacker than coal, too, that black cat was. And it eased over to the fireplace. And it sat right down in the fire. Picked up a red-hot coal in its paws and stuck out its tongue and licked at the coal. Just like lickin some milk, it did too lick that red-hot coal!

John not sayin a word, not payin that cat any mind atall. He had cats at home. But none lived in his house. Nor sat down in a blazin fire and licked up a hot coal. He said his prayers like he was supposed to, but a little faster now.

As quick as a crack of the fire, a long shadow fell over John. It walk around him. The shadow turn out to be a cat, too, only this cat was no kind of house cat. This cat was as big as a huntin dog. Black as coal and his collar fur standin up on his shoulders. The great big cat sat down in the fire and picked up a live, red coal. And he dusts his cheeks with it like that burnin coal just a powder puff. He powders his nose with it, and as proper as you please.

Then that big, ugly cat turn to the first one. He smackin his lips. The big cat says, says, "Are we ready?"

And the first, the regular cat says, says, "We'd better wait till Martin comes."

Well, poor John moves himself then. Has to. But the broken-down chair is weak. Its seat falls in. John is stuck in the chair, can't pull himself out without makin a lot of noise. Somethin tells him to keep still and say his prayers. He says them. He says them as fast as he can, hardly makin a sound. And the big, huntin dog cat and the little, regular cat get on up out of the burnin fire. They stand on the hearth and pat out the smoke. Shake out the ashes. And come on over, sit right down on each side of John.

Poor John stays as still and as twisted up as that haunted tree outside. Sayin his prayers clear through. Whisperin as fast as he can go and not movin his mouth atall.

The next minute there come walkin in behind him and around, a cat twelve times blacker than the other two, and as big as a timber wolf. Bigger. This has to be Martin, John is thinkin, but he won't say a sound. Too scared.

That timber cat walks over and sits down in the fire. Just like the

other cats did it. And he picks up this live coal. And he puts it right on his slanted, green eyes. He dusts his eyeballs with it! And he turns around to the other cats sittin on each side of John.

The timber cat says to the other cats, says, showin his teeth, "What you want to do with him there?" And looks straight dead at John, too.

And the other cats say right back all in one meow, "We better wait till Martin comes."

With that, John gives a great heave up. The chair comes up with him. But at least he was up. And he runs out the wide-open front door. He's callin as he goes out flyin, "Mister Cats! You tell Martin I was here, but I couldn't wait on him. And now I'm gone!"

And he was. Long gone. And never seen in that county since.

This is a comic scare tale, usually told about a preacher. It is an old story, widely known in America among all peoples, and was told for many years on the stage by comedian Bert Williams. The theme of the person who accepts a dare, or decides to stay in a haunted place, is a favorite of the early ghost-tale teller. The animals involved are sometimes monkeys, a gorilla, cats, a timber wolf, a mule, a tiger, or a calf, among others. The huge animal or being for whom the preacher or salesman or simply "I" is too terrified to wait is known in versions of the tale as Emmett, Rufus, John, Martin, Caleb, Whalem-Balem, and Willy, or whatever other name the teller cares to use.

CARRYING THE RUNNING-AWAYS

And Other Slave Tales of Freedom

Carrying the Running-Aways

Never had any idea of carryin the runnin-away slaves over the river. Even though I was right there on the plantation, right by that big river, it never got in my mind to do somethin like that. But one night the woman whose house I had gone courtin to said she knew a pretty girl wanted to cross the river and would I take her. Well, I met the girl and she was awful pretty. And soon the woman was tellin me how to get across, how to go, and when to leave.

Well, I had to think about it. But each day, that girl or the woman would come around, ask me would I row the girl across the river to a place called Ripley. Well, I finally said I would. And one night I went over to the woman's house. My owner trusted me and let me come and go as I pleased, long as I didn't try to read or write anythin. For writin and readin was forbidden to slaves.

Now, I had heard about the other side of the river from the other slaves. But I thought it was just like the side where we lived on the plantation. I thought there were slaves and masters over there, too, and overseers and rawhide whips they used on us. That's why I was so scared. I thought I'd land the girl over there and some overseer didn't know us would beat us for bein out at night. They could do that, you know.

Well, I did it. Oh, it was a long rowin time in the cold, with me worryin. But pretty soon I see a light way up high. Then I remembered the woman told me to watch for a light. Told me to row to the light, which is what I did. And when I got to it, there were two men. They reached down and grabbed the girl. Then one of the men took me by the arm. Said, "You about hungry?" And if he hadn't been holdin me, I would of fell out of that rowboat.

Well, that was my first trip. I was scared for a long time after that. But pretty soon I got over it, as other folks asked me to take them across the river. Two and three at a time, I'd take them. I got used to makin three or four trips every month.

Now it was funny. I never saw my passengers after that first girl. Because I took them on the nights when the moon was not showin, it was cloudy. And I always met them in the open or in a house with no light. So I never saw them, couldn't recognize them, and couldn't

describe them. But I would say to them, "What you say?" And they would say the password. Sounded like "Menare." Seemed the word came from the Bible somewhere, but I don't know. And they would have to say that word before I took them across.

Well, there in Ripley was a man named Mr. Rankins, the rest was John, I think. He had a "station" there for escaping slaves. Ohio was a free state, I found out, so once they got across, Mr. Rankins would see to them. We went at night so we could continue back for more and to be sure no slave catchers would follow us there.

Mr. Rankins had a big light about thirty feet high up and it burned all night. It meant freedom for slaves if they could get to that bright flame.

I worked hard and almost got caught. I'd been rowin fugitives for almost four years. It was in 1863 and it was a night I carried twelve runnin-aways across the river to Mr. Rankins'. I stepped out of the boat back in Kentucky and they were after me. Don't know how they found out. But the slave catchers, didn't know them, were on my trail. I ran away from the plantation and all who I knew there. I lived in the fields and in the woods. Even in caves. Sometimes I slept up in the tree branches. Or in a hay pile. I couldn't get across the river now, it was watched so closely.

Finally, I did get across. Late one night me and my wife went. I had gone back to the plantation to get her. Mr. Rankins had him a bell by this time, along with the light. We were rowin and rowin. We could see the light and hear that bell, but it seemed we weren't gettin any closer. It took forever, it seemed. That was because we were so scared and it was so dark and we knew we could get caught and never get gone.

Well, we did get there. We pulled up there and went on to freedom. It was only a few months before all the slaves was freed.

We didn't stay on at Ripley. We went on to Detroit because I wasn't takin any chances. I have children and grandchildren now. Well, you know, the bigger ones don't care so much to hear about those times. But the little ones, well, they never get tired of hearin how their grandpa brought emancipation to loads of slaves he could touch and feel in the dark but never ever see.

"Carrying the Running-Aways" is a reality tale of freedom, a true slave narrative. The former slave who first told the tale was an actual person, Arnold Gragston, a slave in Kentucky. His story of rowing runaways across the Ohio River represents thousands of such stories of escape to freedom.

The abolitionist who helped the runaways once they were across the river was John Rankin, a Presbyterian minister and a southerner who lived in Ripley, Ohio. The town is still there, situated on the great river. A rickety wood staircase leads up Liberty Hill from Ohio River bottom lands to the Underground "station" house of the Rankin family. From 1825 to 1865, more than two thousand slaves were sheltered at the house and guided on by the family. Today, the Rankin house is a State Memorial open to the public from April through October.

Another fugitive, Levi Perry, born a slave, crossed the Ohio River into freedom with his mother about 1854. They were rescued by John Rankin and were taken in and taken care of at the house with the light. Years later, every six months or so, Levi Perry would settle his ten children around him and he would begin: "Now listen, children. I want to tell you about slavery and how my mother and I ran away from it. So you'll know and never let it happen to you." This tale was told to me recently by my mother, Etta Belle Perry Hamilton, who is 92 years old and Levi Perry's oldest daughter.

How Nehemiah Got Free

In slavery time, there was smart slaves and they did most what they wanted to do by usin just their wits. Hangin around the big house, they kept the slaveowners laughin. They had to "bow and scrape" some, but they often was able to draw the least hard tasks.

Nehemiah was a one who believed that if he must be a slave, he'd best be a smart one. No one who callin himself Master of Nehemiah had ever been able to make him work hard for nothin. Nehemiah would always have a funny lie to tell or he made some laughin remark whenever the so-called Master had a question or a scoldin.

Nehemiah was always bein moved from one plantation to another. For as soon as the slaveowner realized Nehemiah was outwittin him, he sold Nehemiah as quick as he could to some other slaveholder.

One day, the man known as the most cruel slaveowner in that part of the state heard about Nehemiah.

"Oh, I bet I can make that slave do what I tell him to," the slaveowner said. And he went to Nehemiah's owner and bargained for him.

Nehemiah's new owner was Mister Warton, and he told Nehemiah, "I've bought you. Now tomorra, you are goin to work for me over there at my plantation, and you are goin to pick four hundred pounds of cotton a day."

"Well, Mas, suh," Nehemiah says, "that's all right, far as it goes. But if I make you laugh, won't you lemme off for tomorra?"

"Well," said Warton, who had never been known to laugh, "if you make me laugh, I won't only let you off for tomorra, but I'll give you your freedom right then and there!"

"Well, I declare, Mas, suh, you sure a good-lookin man," says Nehemiah.

"I'm sorry I can't say the same about you, Nehemiah," answered the slaveowner.

"Oh, yes, Mas, you could," Nehemiah said, laughin. "You could if you told as big a lie as I just did."

Warton threw back his head and laughed. It was a long, loud bel-

low. He had laughed before he thought. But true is true and facts are facts. And Nehemiah got his freedom.

Folktales about how slaves got their freedom were told in one form or another and are still told in black families all over this country. They are told in the spirit of a Nineteenth of June celebration. That is "Juneteenth," the day on which black people in the South remember Emancipation and give special thanks to freedom from slavery.

Slaves did not learn about Emancipation all at once together. Isolated and scattered all over the South, they heard the extraordinary news at separate times and in different months. But June Nineteenth became the day of freedom for all—Juneteenth. The significance of Juneteenth is very great and gives special meaning to all running-away, enduring-slavery, and end-of-slavery tales.

The Talking Cooter

S ay that Jim was a dreamer. He hoped someday to be a free man. But for now, he was a slave. Not far from the big house of the slaveowner was a pond. Jim liked to sit beside it and think. Someone had told him that animals used to talk. And Jim dreamed that someday some animal would talk to him and tell him how to get his freedom.

One day while Jim was right there by the pond, he spied a big cooter mud turtle at the edge of the water.

Jim picked up a pebble, threw it at the cooter, strikin him on his shell.

The cooter moved aside a little, stuck his head up, and said, "Don't do that again. Let's be frens. Would ya like to hear me play my fiddle?"

Jim was just shocked when the cooter spoke to him. He was most near to fallin over when the cooter took a teeny fiddle from under a stone and commenced to play it.

Jim sat there listenin and thought he just was dreamin. When he came out of his trance, the cooter had gone.

Then, every day, Jim walked over to the pond when his tasks were done. And each day, the cooter would greet him with, "Good mornin, fren. Do ya want to hear me play agin?"

And Jim had found his voice and his wits enough to say, "Yes, indeedy, I do. Good mornin to ya, too, Bruh Cooter."

And then the cooter played his fiddle, and he sang,

> *"Jim, you talk too much.*
> *Run along and find you freedom place."*

Now Jim was a dreamer, but he was a thinker, too. And he thought one day that if he let his owner meet the cooter, he might get his freedom that way. After all, a talkin cooter was a wonderful thing to hear. So Jim went on back to the plantation. He found the slaveowner, and he says, "Mas, I wanter tell you about this cooter down there at the pond."

"Well, what about it?" said the slaveowner.

"Mas," says Jim, "that cooter can talk. And he don't just talk. He taken out his fiddle and he play on it, pretty as you please."

"Oh, get out!" said the slaveowner. "You know that's not true."

"Tis too true," said Jim, as calm as he could. "He speak to me and play and sing for me nearly every day now."

The slaveowner had to laugh. "Well, then, Jim," he said, "if it's true, I'll give you your freedom. But if it's not true, I'm going to give you the worst whippin you ever had in your life."

"That's all right, Mas, I'll show you," said Jim. "I'll take you down there and you'll see for yourself."

So that's what Jim did. He took the slaveowner down to the pond. When they got there, there was no cooter to be seen.

"Huh," grunted the slaveowner. He had his whip in his hand and he snaked it good and hard, making a big, crackin sound.

"Good mornin," Jim said, loud, but not too loud. There was no answer. "Good mornin to ya, cooter," Jim said, a bit louder this time. No answer again.

"Well, I knew it," said the slaveowner. "Dang you, Jim, you fooled with me one time too many!" And he raised his whip to thrash Jim as hard as he could.

Just then, they heard music, a fiddle playin nearby. And right there the cooter came climbin out of the pond. He walked on his back legs and he had that fiddle tucked up under his chin like any ole fiddler. He was playin away on it, too.

"Good mornin," he said, and kept on playin. Then he commenced to sing:

"Jim, I told you you talk too much.
Run along and find you freedom place."

Mebbe Jim did talk too much. But that was how he got his freedom.

The greatest dream or wish of the slave in the Southland was for freedom.
Some of the slave tales show the slave indulging in a wish-fulfilling fantasy of
gaining power over the owner and escaping from him. But it was rare that a
slave won or was given freedom.

"The Talking Cooter" is one of many talking-animal tales with the motif of
"the animal refuses to talk on demand." The talking animal is variously a talking turtle or tortoise or a talking mule. There are other variants, African versions, with talking skulls and bones.

The Riddle Tale of Freedom

Now here it tis. Long time ago, there was a slave and a slaveowner. They got along. They liked to joke back and forth sometimes. Those two would exchange jokes and riddles. The slave man say, "Mas, you give me a riddle today and I figured it out. Now, tomorrow, I'll give you one."

"All right," the slaveowner says, "you bring me one in the mornin."

"And if you can't figure it," said the slave, "you give me my freedom in the mornin, too."

So that was the deal. The mornin come. The slave goes to the owner's place. Owner says, "Come on in. I heard you comin. Come on in. You got that riddle with you you said you'd bring me?"

"Sure do," said the slave. His old dog had died the night before. The dog's name was Love. The slave took a piece of Love's skin and wrapped it around his right hand. So the slave says, "I've got you a riddle right here."

"Well, go ahead," said the owner, "tell it to me."

"Well, then, here," said the slave. And he told the riddle like this:

"Love I see; Love I stand.
Love I holds in my right hand."

"Now what is the answer, Mas?" asked the slave.

The slaveowner thought a long time. He tried to guess the riddle, but he just couldn't figure it out.

"Well, I give up," the slaveowner said. "So I have to give you your freedom because I said I would if I couldn't guess. But first, tell me what the answer is."

"Well, here it tis," said the slave. "See, wrapped around my right hand? That's my dead dog's skin, and his name was Love. Well, I was standin right here with it and I had it in my hand, just seein it. So that's why I tell the riddle:

"Love I see; Love I stand.
Love I holds in my right hand."

That's how the riddle gave the slave his freedom.

Telling riddles was one of the favorite pastimes of slaves. It was second only to telling animal tales. Riddle telling carried on into the Reconstruction period after Emancipation. It became a wish telling about freedom. When one solved the riddle, one would be free.

Here is a typical slave riddle:

Was twelve pear hangin high
An twelve pear hangin low.
Twelve king come ridin by.
Each he took a pear,
An how many leave hangin there?

ANSWER / Begin with, there were twenty-four pears.

A man called Each took one pear.

That left twenty-three pears hangin there.

The Most Useful Slave

Say that John was the most useful slave on the plantation. The slaveowner never havin to worry about his slaves tryin to run away or to startin a bad trouble. He had a way of knowin exactly what was goin on around the plantation. And the way he knew was because of John.

Now John knew how to prophesy for the slaveowner, who was Mas Tom. He could tell you what was gone happen, and he was never wrong once in his predictions. The slaveowner believed John was a fortune-teller with supernatural power. For John knew exactly

: *160*

what the slaveowner wanted done and exactly when he wanted it done, as well.

The truth was that John collected all he needed to know from eavesdroppin, by listenin in on the slaveowner and his wife while they ate their supper.

One day the owner, Tom, was talkin to some other planters, and he found out that they were worried about unrest among the slaves. After listenin awhile, Tom said he never had to worry about anythin because he had a real smart slave who could prophesy.

"There ain't a slave that smart that can foretell," one of the planters said.

"Well, I'll bet you money there is," Tom said.

"You that sure?" the planter asked. And Tom said he was.

"You all put down your money," he told them, "and come over to my house next Sat'dy and you'll see for yourselves."

Well, all the slaveowners put their money down. It came to thousands and thousands of dollars, too. And they all accepted slaveowner Tom's invitation.

Well, the day came. Wasn't a bad day atall. And all the owners came. And they were eager to see this slave that was so smart.

Someone had a place for John to stand. In front of the place one of the planters put a big box. There was something inside it. Nobody knew but the one had put it there what it was.

When everythin seemed to be ready and everybody had gathered around and quieted down, Mas Tom brought John out, blindfolded, and had him stand there.

One of the planters name of Mas Carter said to John, "We're gone see what we see this day, and I got money down on you."

"Well, what for?" blindfolded John says.

"Well, you must know," says the owner Carter. "You the one knows everythin."

Just then, Mas Tom says, "Now, neighbors, Uncle John here will tell us what is hidden in that big box."

Now you know, what was in the big box was a little smaller box so John couldn't hear what was goin on inside.

Well, John stood there for a long, long time, tryin to hear at least some scratchin from the box. But he couldn't. But he worked his hands like he swattin the air and gettin somethin in his head that way. He looked to be tranced some way.

John thought and he thought. The more he had to stand there blindfolded, the more he knew he didn't know what was in the big box. He had no idea atall what was in the little smaller box cause he didn't even know it was there.

It's no use, John thought. Guess what I will is in that box, I'd be wrong. "In the box! In the box!" he said out loud. Didn't know he'd said it. But it caused the planters there to get to murmurin, thinkin somethin was about to happen. He'd said "box" twice, and that made the owner Carter take a listen.

And John was figurin he might as well give it up. He scratched his head and shifted his feet around.

"Well, Mas Tom," he said finally, "this old raccoon, he run a long time, but they caught him at last."

When John said that, his owner, Tom, lifted the box and the smaller box. Lo and behold, a raccoon jumped out to the ground.

"Well, thank you, Uncle John!" says his owner. He couldn't've been happier. See, John was a prophet and Mas Tom was a whole bunch richer.

John doesn't get his freedom in this tale, but he will be valued so long as he can continue as "the prophet." This is the best-known of the "old Marster and John (or Jack)" or "old Marster and the slave" tales, of which there are many.

Old Marster, sometimes called Mas, and John tales are found in the southern United States and among East Africans, and Haitians, Jamaicans, Puerto Ricans, and many other Caribbean peoples. The tales are a cycle narrative (tales told one after the other over a period of time), sometimes accompanied by the banjo. They reveal the slave, John, rather than Bruh Rabbit, as the plantation slaves' trickster hero. John and the owner seem to have an almost friendly relationship.

In some of the other John tales, Old Mas is referred to as Boss, which identifies those tales as taking place after slavery and signals the former slave's uneasy relationship with his former owner.

The People Could Fly

They say the people could fly. Say that long ago in Africa, some of the people knew magic. And they would walk up on the air like climbin up on a gate. And they flew like blackbirds over the fields. Black, shiny wings flappin against the blue up there.

Then, many of the people were captured for Slavery. The ones that could fly shed their wings. They couldn't take their wings across the water on the slave ships. Too crowded, don't you know.

The folks were full of misery, then. Got sick with the up and down of the sea. So they forgot about flyin when they could no longer breathe the sweet scent of Africa.

Say the people who could fly kept their power, although they shed their wings. They kept their secret magic in the land of slavery. They looked the same as the other people from Africa who had been coming over, who had dark skin. Say you couldn't tell anymore one who could fly from one who couldn't.

One such who could was an old man, call him Toby. And standin tall, yet afraid, was a young woman who once had wings. Call her Sarah. Now Sarah carried a babe tied to her back. She trembled to be so hard worked and scorned.

The slaves labored in the fields from sunup to sundown. The owner of the slaves callin himself their Master. Say he was a hard lump of clay. A hard, glinty coal. A hard rock pile, wouldn't be moved. His Overseer on horseback pointed out the slaves who were slowin down. So the one called Driver cracked his whip over the slow ones to make them move faster. That whip was a slice-open cut of pain. So they did move faster. Had to.

Sarah hoed and chopped the row as the babe on her back slept.

Say the child grew hungry. That babe started up bawling too loud. Sarah couldn't stop to feed it. Couldn't stop to soothe and quiet it down. She let it cry. She didn't want to. She had no heart to croon to it.

"Keep that thing quiet," called the Overseer. He pointed his finger at the babe. The woman scrunched low. The Driver cracked his whip across the babe anyhow. The babe hollered like any hurt child, and the woman fell to the earth.

The old man that was there, Toby, came and helped her to her feet.

"I must go soon," she told him.

"Soon," he said.

Sarah couldn't stand up straight any longer. She was too weak. The sun burned her face. The babe cried and cried, "Pity me, oh, pity me," say it sounded like. Sarah was so sad and starvin, she sat down in the row.

"Get up, you black cow," called the Overseer. He pointed his hand, and the Driver's whip snarled around Sarah's legs. Her sack dress tore into rags. Her legs bled onto the earth. She couldn't get up.

Toby was there where there was no one to help her and the babe.

"Now, before it's too late," panted Sarah. "Now, Father!"

"Yes, Daughter, the time is come," Toby answered. "Go, as you know how to go!"

He raised his arms, holding them out to her. *"Kum . . . yali, kum buba tambe,"* and more magic words, said so quickly, they sounded like whispers and sighs.

The young woman lifted one foot on the air. Then the other. She flew clumsily at first, with the child now held tightly in her arms. Then she felt the magic, the African mystery. Say she rose just as free as a bird. As light as a feather.

The Overseer rode after her, hollerin. Sarah flew over the fences. She flew over the woods. Tall trees could not snag her. Nor could the Overseer. She flew like an eagle now, until she was gone from sight. No one dared speak about it. Couldn't believe it. But it was, because they that was there saw that it was.

Say the next day was dead hot in the fields. A young man slave fell from the heat. The Driver come and whipped him. Toby come over and spoke words to the fallen one. The words of ancient Africa once heard are never remembered completely. The young man forgot them as soon as he heard them. They went way inside him. He got up and rolled over on the air. He rode it awhile. And he flew away.

Another and another fell from the heat. Toby was there. He cried out to the fallen and reached his arms out to them. *"Kum kunka yali, kum . . . tambe!"* Whispers and sighs. And they too rose on the air. They rode the hot breezes. The ones flyin were black and shinin sticks, wheelin above the head of the Overseer. They crossed the rows, the fields, the fences, the streams, and were away.

"Seize the old man!" cried the Overseer. "I heard him say the magic *words.* Seize him!"

The one callin himself Master come runnin. The Driver got his whip ready to curl around old Toby and tie him up. The slaveowner took his hip gun from its place. He meant to kill old, black Toby.

But Toby just laughed. Say he threw back his head and said, "Hee, hee! Don't you know who I am? Don't you know some of us in this field?" He said it to their faces. "We are ones who fly!"

And he sighed the ancient words that were a dark promise. He said them all around to the others in the field under the whip, "*. . . buba yali . . . buba tambe. . . .*"

There was a great outcryin. The bent backs straighted up. Old and young who were called slaves and could fly joined hands. Say like they would ring-sing. But they didn't shuffle in a circle. They didn't sing. They rose on the air. They flew in a flock that was black against the heavenly blue. Black crows or black shadows. It didn't matter, they went so high. Way above the plantation, way over the slavery land. Say they flew away to *Free-dom.*

And the old man, old Toby, flew behind them, takin care of them. He wasn't cryin. He wasn't laughin. He was the seer. His gaze fell on the plantation where the slaves who could not fly waited.

"*Take us with you!*" Their looks spoke it but they were afraid to shout it. Toby couldn't take them with him. Hadn't the time to teach them to fly. They must wait for a chance to run.

"Goodie-bye!" The old man called Toby spoke to them, poor souls! And he was flyin gone.

So they say. The Overseer told it. The one called Master said it was a lie, a trick of the light. The Driver kept his mouth shut.

The slaves who could not fly told about the people who could fly to their children. When they were free. When they sat close before the fire in the free land, they told it. They did so love firelight and *Free-dom,* and tellin.

They say that the children of the ones who could not fly told their children. And now, me, I have told it to you.

"The People Could Fly" is one of the most extraordinary, moving tales in black folklore. It almost makes us believe that the people *could* fly. There are numerous separate accounts of flying Africans and slaves in the black folktale literature. Such accounts are often combined with tales of slaves disappearing. A plausible explanation might be the slaves running away from slavery, slipping away while in the fields or under cover of darkness. In code language murmured from one slave to another, "Come fly away!" might have been the words used. Another explanation is the wish-fulfillment motif.

The magic hoe variant is often combined with the flying-African tale. A magic hoe is left still hoeing in an empty field after all the slaves have flown away. Magic with the hoe and other farm tools, and the power of disappearing, are often attributed to Gullah (Angolan) African slaves. Angolan slaves were thought by other slaves to have exceptional powers.

"The People Could Fly" is a detailed fantasy tale of suffering, of magic power exerted against the so-called Master and his underlings. Finally, it is a powerful testament to the millions of slaves who never had the opportunity to "fly" away. They remained slaves, as did their children. "The People Could Fly" was first told and retold by those who had only their imaginations to set them free.

Bibliography

The folktales are told in many ways by a number of storytellers. Other versions can be found in some of the books listed below.

Abrahams, Roger. *Deep Down in the Jungle . . .: Negro Narrative Folklore from the Streets of Philadelphia.* Hatboro, Pa.: Folklore Associates, 1964.

Aswell, James R., et al. *Tennessee Writers' Project.* Chapel Hill, N.C.: The University of North Carolina Press, 1960.

Beckwith, Martha Warren. *Black Roadways.* Chapel Hill, N.C.: The University of North Carolina Press, 1929.

Bennett, John. *The Doctor to the Dead: Grotesque Legends & Folk Tales of Old Charleston.* New York: Rinehart & Company, Inc., 1943.

Botkin, B.A., ed. *Lay My Burden Down: A Folk History of Slavery*. Original material, Federal Works Project of the Works Progress Administration, 1939. Chicago: University of Chicago Press, 1945.

———, ed. *A Treasury of American Folklore*. New York: Crown Publishers, Inc., 1944.

———, ed. *A Treasury of Southern Folklore*. New York: Crown Publishers, Inc., 1949.

Brewer, John Mason. *Worser Days and Better Times: Tales of the Wise and Foolish, the Folklore of the North Carolina Negro*. Chicago: Quadrangle Books, 1965.

Cox, John Harrington. "Negro Tales from West Virginia," in *Journal of American Folklore*, Vol. 47, 1934, New York.

Davis, Henry C. "Negro Folk-Lore in South Carolina," in *Journal of American Folk-Lore*, Vol. 27, 1914.

Dobie, J. F., ed. *Tone the Bell Easy*. Austin, Texas: Texas Folklore Society, 1932.

Dorson, Richard M. *American Negro Folktales*. Bloomington, Ind.: Indiana University Press, 1958; New York: Fawcett Books, A Fawcett Premier Original, 1967.

Drums and Shadows: Survival Studies Among the Georgia Coastal Negroes. By the Savannah Unit of the Georgia Writers' Project of the Works Progress Administration. Athens, Georgia: University of Georgia Press, 1940; reprint: Westport, Conn.: Greenwood Press, 1973.

Dubois, W.E.B. *The Suppression of the African Slave-Trade to the United States of America 1638-1870*. "Portugal," "Slaves in Colonies," "Abolition of Slave-Trade," "Treaties with England, 1869, 1870," "Bill on Slave Trade, 1871." Reissue: New York: Schocken Books, 1969.

Fauset, Arthur Huff. "Negro Folk Tales from the South (Alabama, Mississippi, Louisiana)," in *Journal of American Folklore*, Vol. 40, 1927.

Fortier, Alcee. "Louisiana Folk-Tales," in *Memoirs of the American Folklore Society*, Vol. 2, 1895.

Gonzales, Ambrose Elliot. *The Black Border: Gullah Stories of the Carolina Coast (with a Glossary)*. Columbia, S.C.: The State Company, 1922.

Harris, Joel Chandler. *Uncle Remus, His Songs and His Sayings: The Folklore of the Old Plantation*. New York: Appleton-Century Company, 1881.

Hughes, Langston, and Arna Bontemps, eds. *Book of Negro Folk-Lore*. New York: Dodd, Mead & Company, 1958.

Hurston, Zora Neale. *Mules and Men.* Philadelphia: J.B. Lippincott, 1935; new edition: Bloomington, Ind.: Indiana University Press, 1978.

Jamison, C. V. "Alabama Legend Concerning the Will-o'-the-Wisp," in *Journal of American Folk-Lore,* Vol. 18, 1905.

Jones, Charles C. *Negro Myths from the Georgia Coast, Told in the Vernacular.* Boston and New York: Houghton, Mifflin, 1888; reissue: Detroit: Singing Tree Press, 1969.

Long, Andrew. *Custom and Myth.* London, 1901.

Odum, Howard W. *Cold Blue Moon: Black Ulysses Afar Off.* Indianapolis: The Bobbs-Merrill Company, 1931.

Parsons, Elsie Clews, coll. "Folklore from the Cape Verde Islands," in *Memoirs of the American Folk-Lore Society,* Vol. 15, Part I, No. 18. Cambridge, Mass: The Cosmos Press, Inc., 1923.

————"Folk-Lore of the Sea Islands, South Carolina," in *Memoirs of the American Folk-Lore Society, Vol.* 26, 1943.

————"Tales from Guildford County, North Carolina," in *Journal of American Folk-Lore,* Vol. 30, 1917, and Vol. 34, 1921.

Pendleton, L. "Notes on Negro Folk-Lore and Witchcraft in the South," in *Journal of American Folk-Lore,* Vol. 3, 1890.

Percy, William Alexander. *Lanterns on the Levee: Recollections of a Planter's Son.* New York: Alfred A Knopf, Inc., 1941.

Porter, Kenneth. "Flying Africans," reprinted in *Common Ground: Primer for White Folks,* ed. by Bucklin Moon. Garden City, N.Y.: Doubleday, Doran and Co., Inc., 1945.

Puckett, Newbell Niles. *Folk Beliefs of the Southern Negro.* Chapell Hill, N.C.: The University of North Carolina Press, 1926.

Randolph, Vance. *The Devil's Pretty Daughter and Other Ozark Folk Tales.* New York: Columbia University Press, 1955.

Stoney, Samuel Gaillard, and Gertrude Mathews Shelby. *Black Genesis.* New York: The Macmillan Company, 1930.

Talley, Thomas W. *Negro Folk Rhymes.* New York: The Macmillan Company, 1922.

Van de Voort, Donnell, coll. "Wiley and the Hairy Man." The Manuscripts of the

Federal Writers' Project of the Works Progress Administration for the State of Alabama.

Whitney, Annie W., and Caroline C. Bullock. *Folk-Lore From Maryland. Memoirs of the American Folk-Lore Society,* Vol. 18, 1925, New York.

VIRGINIA HAMILTON

is one of our most distinguished writers for children. In addition to the Newbery Medal, she has won the National Book Award, the Coretta Scott King Award (twice), the *Boston Globe–Horn Book* Award, and most recently, the Hans Christian Andersen Medal. She is married to the poet Arnold Adoff and lives in Yellow Springs, Ohio.

LEO *and* DIANE DILLON

have twice won the Caldecott Medal; their work is associated with some of the most beautiful books ever published for children. They live in Brooklyn, New York.